FOOD
Retail Design & Display 3

FOOD
Retail Design & Display 3

Edited by Martin M. Pegler, SVM

RETAIL REPORTING CORPORATION • NEW YORK

Copyright © 1994 by Retail Reporting Corporation

All rights reserved. No part of this book may be reproduced in any form, by mimeograph or any other means, without permission in writing from the publisher.

Retail Reporting Corporation
302 Fifth Avenue
New York, NY 10001

Distributors to the trade in the United States and Canada
Van Nostrand Reinhold
115 Fifth Avenue
New York, NY 10003

Distributors outside the United States and Canada
Hearst Books International
1350 Avenue of the Americas
New York, NY 10019

Library of Congress Cataloging in Publication Data:
Food: Retail Design & Display / 3

Printed in Hong Kong
ISBN 0-934590-61-3

Designed by Bernard Schleifer

Contents

INTRODUCTION..7

MARKETS &
SPECIALTY
FOOD SHOPS..10

COFFEE BARS,
COFFEE SHOPS,
COFFEE STORES
& CAFES..50

CAFETERIAS &
SELF-SERVICE
FOOD AREAS..88

INFORMAL &
THEMATIC DINING......................................118

INTERNATIONAL
FLAVORS &
EXHIBITION
KITCHENS..160

FOOD COURTS
& FAST FOOD
CONCESSIONS...206

Introduction

"It is part of a wise man to feed himself with moderate, pleasant food and drink, and to take pleasure with perfumes, with the beauty of growing plants, dress, music, sports and theater — and other places of this kind which man may use without hurt to his fellows." Way back in the 17th Century, the philosopher Benedict Spinoza wrote these words which could describe "dining out" and also be the anthem for what the retail design of food areas is all about. Food presentation takes in the product and the setting in which the food is shown; it is a matter of creating a time and a place — a setting that compliments the product being offered as well as the customer/diner who desires to partake of the offering.

Presentation is dedicated to all the senses. Shoppers/diners are asked to "take pleasure with the perfumes" of food freshly prepared or just baked; to enjoy the "theater" of the preparation of the food whether it is in a marketplace, a gourmet food shop or in an exhibition kitchen which is filled with action — with light and the drama of creation. Markets, stores, cafes, fast food operations and self-service restaurants combine light and color to affect the settings for the foods and then the settings are enhanced for the customer/consumer with "the beauty of growing plants," trees and sometimes even a few fresh daisies in a Perrier bottle. Along with the perfumes of cooked and baked foods, the air is filled with the sound of music that is conducive to dining or to making selections in specialty food stores. Food presentation is sight, smell, sound, and touch — and then the ultimate sense — the sense of taste.

With this edition of Food: Retail Design & Display we have extended even further our perimeters to include more European and Asian projects from outdoor farmer's markets to deluxe food shops and to dining environments where the elements of "theater" are so important. There are the wonderful and colorful markets in Hungary and Vienna where, with simple and naive presentation techniques, they make the sophisticated shopper stop and want to taste — and buy everything. We have included the true boulangeries and charcuteries of France; simple, provincial and honest, but with the innate knowledge of how to display the merchandise — what colors and textures to use — what food to set alongside what other food — what lighting will make the food seem most attractive. The Rustic or Country-style clichés that are often attempted in the design of up-scaled, urban "gourmet" shops is inherent in these local shops designed for the locals. We have also included the world-famous Kafer store in Munich — the unbelievable food shops in department stores and even a Hong Kong-style market/food shop located in NYC's Soho district.

Coffee stores, shops, stands, bars, and also cafes, have proliferated in the last few years in the U.S. The Seattle "coffee shop" trend has swept eastward along with shoppers' demands for more unusual and special blends of coffee and tea. Following up on the noted Seattle operations that we showed in Books 1 and 2, we now add some noted newcomers such as Pasqua, Seattle Coffee Roasters, and New World Coffee, as well as the well-established Barnie's Coffee stores and stands that are familiar landmarks in the better malls across the country. We have also included examples from Vienna, Munich, Cologne, Berlin, London, Paris, Nara in Japan, and Helsinki. This is truly the International setting!

The International note continues in the chapter on "Cafeterias and Self-Serve" operations and the chapter on "Informal & Theme Dining." "International Flavors and Exhibition Kitchens" shows our fascination with foreign or ethnic foods and how these foods are prepared. The open or exhibition kitchen is more than a place of preparation; it is an arena — a stage full of action and movement — of flashing knives, gleaming pots and pans — steam and smoke — the sizzle of meats on spits — the aroma of wood burning grills and ovens. It is the fun of eating food with foreign accents and often fiery seasonings. It is like traveling without ever actually leaving home.

The food courts we highlight are located in different parts of the U.S. and we have included two new large malls in England. The fast food stands we've selected reflect some of the trends that are appearing in the vendor operations in the food courts.

There is no simple answer to the question posed by Louis Untermeyer at the turn of the century:

> "Why has our poetry eschewed
> The rapture and response of Food?"

It has to do with presentation; how it looks and smells before it is even tasted.

> "What hymns are sung, what praises said,
> For home made miracles of bread."

It is the smell of freshly-brewed coffee — buns and breads still steaming as they leave the ovens — the skewered meats off spits or revolving rotisseries — the aromas and perfumes that fill the store, the shop, the food court, that are the "hymns" and "praises" and that also create the retail setting for food.

Martin M. Pegler

FOOD
Retail Design & Display 3

Markets & Specialty Food Shops

Ben's Kosher Deli & Restaurant
Bayside, NY

Ben's Kosher Deli & Restaurant

Bayside, NY

Architect: Stephen Sanders & Associates-Architecture & Interiors, Manhasset, NY
Lead Designer: Kevin Maher
Project Architect: Craig Westergard
Construction Manager: Peter Pizzillo
Photographer: Gil Amiaga

This new restaurant is the latest addition to the successful Long Island and New York chain of Ben's Kosher Delis, located in the new Bay Terrace Shopping Center. The 3800 sq. ft. space was planned to have three distinct focus areas; the deli counter, the main level dining room and the raised skylit garden terrace. The owner, Ronald Dragoon directed his architect, Stephen Sanders to design a store that would re-define the traditional delicatessen dining experience; a place that would be sophisticated, fun to be in, and enhance the food as well.

After passing thru the vestibule with a menu monitor showing the day's specials, one is immediately greeted by the powerful sculptured stainless steel and glass deli counter and spectacular display of food. The streamlined forms of the counter with its lit, carved glass wave and star motif, horizontal lines of the menu board and light forms, direct the hungry crowds to the dining areas beyond. The sweeping shapes in the terrazzo floor also guides you back.

Straight ahead past the revolving dessert case, one enters the main dining space with its domed trompe l'oeil ceiling in which there is a silver and gold leaf non-denominational star and a five-foot diameter alabaster chandelier. The starburst is reflected on the floor by the terrazzo design. All the tables are custom designed from a marble-like composite material. The booths against the walls are punctuated by peach mirrored "windows" with faux marble frames, modernistic hanging lights and the upholstered banquettes have a checkerboard pattern of silver and gold. A decorative functional display wall of mirror and glass separates the dining room from the main service areas. Visibility of the dining room from the service area is monitored thru the decorative circular window.

The upper level garden terrace with its lacewood and moire stainless steel checkerboard wall, and flowing stepped cover lit ceiling with skylight has a free spirit feeling. The central tri-shaped planter creates more intimacy within the space. The revolving column with the bronze armillary sundial extending above the planter towards the skylight adds to the dynamics of the space. The pink diffused neon casts a flattering glow of warmth and richness.

Introduction

"It is part of a wise man to feed himself with moderate, pleasant food and drink, and to take pleasure with perfumes, with the beauty of growing plants, dress, music, sports and theater — and other places of this kind which man may use without hurt to his fellows." Way back in the 17th Century, the philosopher Benedict Spinoza wrote these words which could describe "dining out" and also be the anthem for what the retail design of food areas is all about. Food presentation takes in the product and the setting in which the food is shown; it is a matter of creating a time and a place — a setting that compliments the product being offered as well as the customer/diner who desires to partake of the offering.

Presentation is dedicated to all the senses. Shoppers/diners are asked to "take pleasure with the perfumes" of food freshly prepared or just baked; to enjoy the "theater" of the preparation of the food whether it is in a marketplace, a gourmet food shop or in an exhibition kitchen which is filled with action — with light and the drama of creation. Markets, stores, cafes, fast food operations and self-service restaurants combine light and color to affect the settings for the foods and then the settings are enhanced for the customer/consumer with "the beauty of growing plants," trees and sometimes even a few fresh daisies in a Perrier bottle. Along with the perfumes of cooked and baked foods, the air is filled with the sound of music that is conducive to dining or to making selections in specialty food stores. Food presentation is sight, smell, sound, and touch — and then the ultimate sense — the sense of taste.

With this edition of Food: Retail Design & Display we have extended even further our perimeters to include more European and Asian projects from outdoor farmer's markets to deluxe food shops and to dining environments where the elements of "theater" are so important. There are the wonderful and colorful markets in Hungary and Vienna where, with simple and naive presentation techniques, they make the sophisticated shopper stop and want to taste — and buy everything. We have included the true boulangeries and charcuteries of France; simple, provincial and honest, but with the innate knowledge of how to display the merchandise — what colors and textures to use — what food to set alongside what other food — what lighting will make the food seem most attractive. The Rustic or Country-style clichés that are often attempted in the design of up-scaled, urban "gourmet" shops is inherent in these local shops designed for the locals. We have also included the world-famous Kafer store in Munich — the unbelievable food shops in department stores and even a Hong Kong-style market/food shop located in NYC's Soho district.

Coffee stores, shops, stands, bars, and also cafes, have proliferated in the last few years in the U.S. The Seattle "coffee shop" trend has swept eastward along with shoppers' demands for more unusual and special blends of coffee and tea. Following up on the noted Seattle operations that we showed in Books 1 and 2, we now add some noted newcomers such as Pasqua, Seattle Coffee Roasters, and New World Coffee, as well as the well-established Barnie's Coffee stores and stands that are familiar landmarks in the better malls across the country. We have also included examples from Vienna, Munich, Cologne, Berlin, London, Paris, Nara in Japan, and Helsinki. This is truly the International setting!

The International note continues in the chapter on "Cafeterias and Self-Serve" operations and the chapter on "Informal & Theme Dining." "International Flavors and Exhibition Kitchens" shows our fascination with foreign or ethnic foods and how these foods are prepared. The open or exhibition kitchen is more than a place of preparation; it is an arena — a stage full of action and movement — of flashing knives, gleaming pots and pans — steam and smoke — the sizzle of meats on spits — the aroma of wood burning grills and ovens. It is the fun of eating food with foreign accents and often fiery seasonings. It is like traveling without ever actually leaving home.

The food courts we highlight are located in different parts of the U.S. and we have included two new large malls in England. The fast food stands we've selected reflect some of the trends that are appearing in the vendor operations in the food courts.

There is no simple answer to the question posed by Louis Untermeyer at the turn of the century:

> *"Why has our poetry eschewed*
> *The rapture and response of Food?"*

It has to do with presentation; how it looks and smells before it is even tasted.

> *"What hymns are sung, what praises said,*
> *For home made miracles of bread."*

It is the smell of freshly-brewed coffee — buns and breads still steaming as they leave the ovens — the skewered meats off spits or revolving rotisseries — the aromas and perfumes that fill the store, the shop, the food court, that are the "hymns" and "praises" and that also create the retail setting for food.

Martin M. Pegler

FOOD

Retail Design & Display 3

Markets & Specialty Food Shops

Ben's Kosher Deli & Restaurant
Bayside, NY

BEN'S KOSHER DELI & RESTAURANT

Bayside, NY

*Architect: Stephen Sanders & Associates-Architecture & Interiors,
Manhasset, NY*
Lead Designer: Kevin Maher
Project Architect: Craig Westergard
Construction Manager: Peter Pizzillo
Photographer: Gil Amiaga

This new restaurant is the latest addition to the successful Long Island and New York chain of Ben's Kosher Delis, located in the new Bay Terrace Shopping Center. The 3800 sq. ft. space was planned to have three distinct focus areas; the deli counter, the main level dining room and the raised skylit garden terrace. The owner, Ronald Dragoon directed his architect, Stephen Sanders to design a store that would re-define the traditional delicatessen dining experience; a place that would be sophisticated, fun to be in, and enhance the food as well.

After passing thru the vestibule with a menu monitor showing the day's specials, one is immediately greeted by the powerful sculptured stainless steel and glass deli counter and spectacular display of food. The streamlined forms of the counter with its lit, carved glass wave and star motif, horizontal lines of the menu board and light forms, direct the hungry crowds to the dining areas beyond. The sweeping shapes in the terrazzo floor also guides you back.

Straight ahead past the revolving dessert case, one enters the main dining space with its domed trompe l'oeil ceiling in which there is a silver and gold leaf non-denominational star and a five-foot diameter alabaster chandelier. The starburst is reflected on the floor by the terrazzo design. All the tables are custom designed from a marble-like composite material. The booths against the walls are punctuated by peach mirrored "windows" with faux marble frames, modernistic hanging lights and the upholstered banquettes have a checkerboard pattern of silver and gold. A decorative functional display wall of mirror and glass separates the dining room from the main service areas. Visibility of the dining room from the service area is monitored thru the decorative circular window.

The upper level garden terrace with its lacewood and moire stainless steel checkerboard wall, and flowing stepped cover lit ceiling with skylight has a free spirit feeling. The central tri-shaped planter creates more intimacy within the space. The revolving column with the bronze armillary sundial extending above the planter towards the skylight adds to the dynamics of the space. The pink diffused neon casts a flattering glow of warmth and richness.

If one had to label the style of the design, since many do ask, it probably can be called eclectic, art moderne, art deco, nostalgic. What it really is, is a new, classy fun deli design. All the rest is baloney.

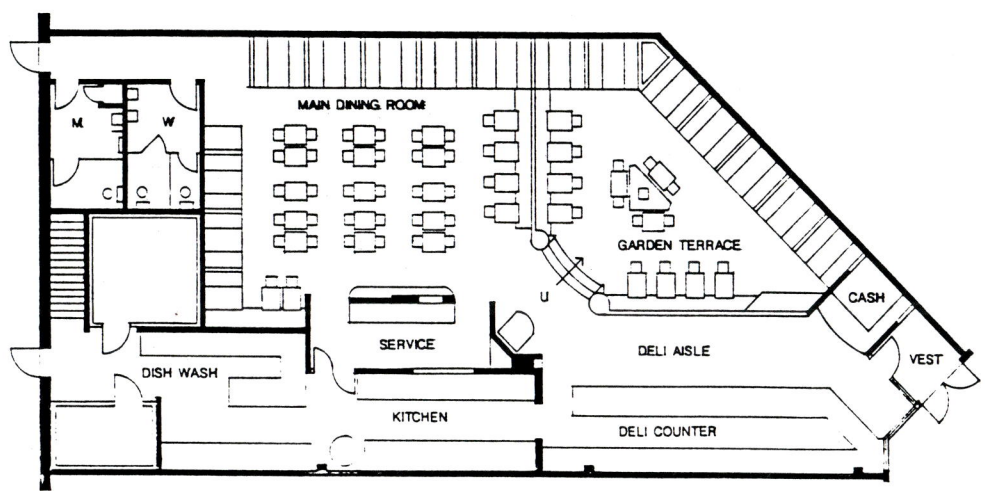

Abda Market
Abda, Hungary

Outdoor markets are as old and as traditional as time. Farmers have always brought their produce and products to the open squares or marketplaces where they have displayed them with love and pride. That tradition still exists in many areas of the world, today, enhanced somewhat by modern technology and building crafts. We open this chapter with two outdoor markets — each famous in its own way.

As the shopper or traveler leaves Hungary, just before the border, he or she will go through the town of Abda. The town is one long marketplace since all along the highway — for almost a mile — it is shop after shop — stand after stand brimming over and gushing out into the road with wealth of the land. In a country that has only recently reverted to democracy, it is the capitalistic way that appears with competition spurring on each shopkeeper who makes the journey down this food-filled route such a colorful spectacle.

In addition to the fruits and vegetables, the garlands of pearly garlic, the displays of paprika (sweet or hot), the festoons of fiery dried red peppers, there are the salamis, the preserved dried meats, the assorted native cheeses, the freshly baked breads and the home made preserves displayed along with familiar liters of Sprite, Pepsi, and Coca Cola in their plastic containers.

The boxes of produce are beautifully arranged with colors contrasting and textures juxtaposed — with the innate knowledge of the shopkeepers as to what it takes to properly present their wares.

The corrugated aluminum and steel girder sheds are simple, unadorned — totally utilitarian except for the wares which provide the stimuli that can stop a car or bus. People travel especially into Abda across the irksome, irritating and the time consuming petty provincial patrolled border just to share in this wealth from Hungarian farms and farmers.

Photographer: MMP/RVC

When sunlight alone won't do, incandescent lamps unceremoniously screwed into the metal ceilings add to the full rich color of the produce and products.

Nasch Markt
Vienna, Austria

In the sophisticated city of Vienna — the city of fine and elegant shops — of the Opera House — of art nouveau apartment buildings and grandiose Metro stations designed by Otto Wagner at the turn of the last century, there is a half mile stretch of open market girded by enclosed stands, stalls, and shops that is familiarly known by the natives as The Nasch Markt.

To "nasch" is to indulge — to sample and taste — to pick up and walk on. To stroll along this market is to visit the many countries whose people now live in Vienna for it is an international gastronomic excursion past stalls filled with native foods and delicacies as well as imported ones such as olives, dates, figs, halvah, cheeses, and dried meats, breads, and cakes — freshly baked — that one would expect to see in bakeries in Greece, Turkey, Southern Russia, and in the Near East.

Though most of the stalls show off their age as do the windowed shops — and the age for many is almost 100 years, there is an immediacy and vitality about the market. Not only are shoppers stopping to select, touch, smell, feel — to argue the price and eventually buy and stuff the purchase into string bags or woven baskets worn over the arm, they are also "sampling" or "nasching" on the wares.

The market is an island of food between two major trafficked streets with a Metro running along side and below it. The aromas of the freshly baked goods mingle with that of the pickles, sauerkraut, herbs and spices sold by the kilo; there is the color of the foods and produce, and over all, the cacophony of accents and dialects of the vendors as they shout out their wares. One is tempted to buy anything and everything because everything looks so wonderfully fresh and nasch-able. For those who want to "picnic" on foot, the Nasch Markt is the ultimate destination where the world of food is assembled in a colorful hodge podge that stimulates all of the senses.

AGATHA & VALENTINA
New York, NY

In a change of venue, we travel from Europe to New York — and in a way — right back to Europe. The designers of Agatha & Valentina took their inspiration from markets in Sicily and made use of inherently Sicilian design motifs and architectural elements to recreate an Old World setting.

The architects traveled to Sicily to immerse themselves and to also document the feeling of the country. While there they selected materials which would be used in the construction of the shop. "The design, as it is, an amalgamation of Sicilian design tempered by the functional requirements necessitated by a gourmet food market." A "teglia" — an Italian tile canopy — delineates the perimeter of the store. Small shops in Sicily often have just such curved tile projections extending out over there exposed wares, and here the continuous band around the store turns the central area into an open marketplace surrounded by "enclosed" stalls.

The market concept is further enhanced with a native style hanging wood trellis which is used in several areas for the display of food products such as cheese, dried meats, salamis, and such.

Though the store is "dynamic and full of activity" — like a marketplace, the designers also provided some "quiet" spaces for the shoppers such as the Cappuccino bar with seating up near the front of the store. It is a focal point that is easily seen along with the rest of the store through the expanse of glass in the storefront. "We felt it was critical to open the store and entice patrons in."

"Activity, pageantry, color and design create interest," and add to the visual excitement of the store along with the mouth-watering aromas that fill the space since all the cooking and preparation is done out in the open — under the teglia.

This very contemporary gourmet food emporium stresses the quality of the fresh foods and by using traditionally Sicilian materials, artifacts and design elements, the architects have created a truly Sicilian market in the heart of New York City.

Architect: Cybul & Cybul, Edgewater, NJ
Martin Cybul
Custom Millwork: Commercial Displays & Designs, Norwich, NY
Photographer: Scott Weitz, Norwich, NY

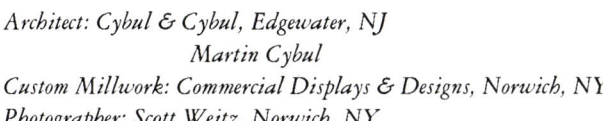

Island Market at Fisher Island

Fisher Island, FL

Fisher Island is a private community in Miami's Biscayne Bay and the Island Market was "created in the fine tradition of European gourmet markets" for the residents of the up-scaled Fisher Island.

The 3500 sq. ft. remodel of an existing store included a new main entrance which incorporates a series of old fashioned bay windows — each one features a fabulous display of different epicurean delights. "Shoppers enter into a world of culinary pleasures as they experience the sights, sounds and aromas of this unique gourmet marketplace." The light and airy Mediterranean feeling of this market was inspired by the historic Vanderbilt Mansion which is a 1920s villa of Mediterranean styling that is found here on Fisher Island.

Fossil stone arches, terra cotta tile floors and polished marble counters trimmed with gleaming brass provide the "old world" ambience for the specialty foods. Custom wood fixtures and hand crafted wrought iron baker's racks are used to hold and display the merchandise. The "old world" brass and glass chandeliers are incorporated with the signage program of the store and they hold the information about the area below the fixture. The signage makes it easy for the first-time shopper to experience the whole elegant presentation of wines, pastries, gourmet foods and fresh tropical fruits. Shopping Island Market is truly a unique and up-scaled food shopping experience.

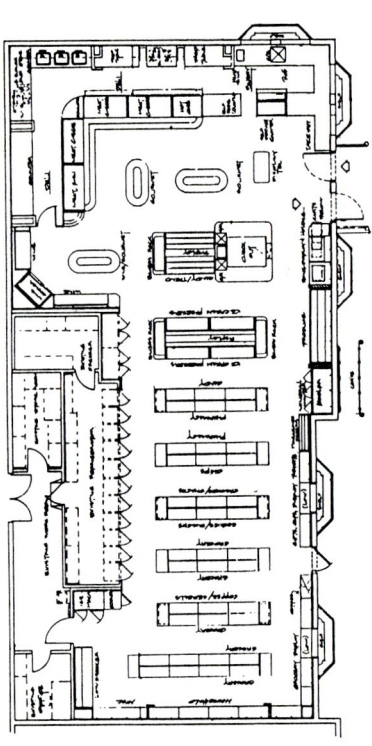

Design: Pavlik Design Team, Ft. Lauderdale, FL

Neuman & Bogdonoff
New York, NY

Located on the upper east sside of New York — a fashionable area — is the Neuman & Bogdonoff Gourmet Food Store. For over ten years, the company has successfully operated the catering/specialty food store in the narrow 760 sq. ft. space. When opportunity allowed them to expand their operation into the adjoining space which permitted them to almost double the space (1760 sq. ft.), they called upon Pentagram Design, an architectural/graphics firm, to "transform the shop from a specialty food boutique to a full service neighborhood market complete with cheese counters and fresh produce cases."

The designers borrowed elements from the local American Deli, the French charcuterie and the elegant English food halls. Thus, the space is filled with bright, clear lighting, white tiles and grand — though somewhat flattened — arches in a space with limited height. "Classical and understated, the interior is a stage on which fresh and packaged foods are displayed to their best advantage." The flecked white terrazzo floor is accented with black triangles and the walls are partly sheathed with large white tile squares that are bordered in black. The arches and the ceilings above the white tiled areas are painted a yellow vanilla color and white milk glass covered drop lights are suspended from the ceiling. There are also tracks on the ceiling for the movable spots that are used to highlight the merchandise presented on the antique white and natural pine, provincial style tables that also help to define the traffic pattern in the store which now "ells" off into the adjoining space.

The new storefront design encompasses the original entrance plus the addition and "bold graphics were designed for the shop front and awning to increase the shop's presence at street level." The dark hunter green and stainless steel trim reinforce the elegance viewed through the expansive glass show windows.

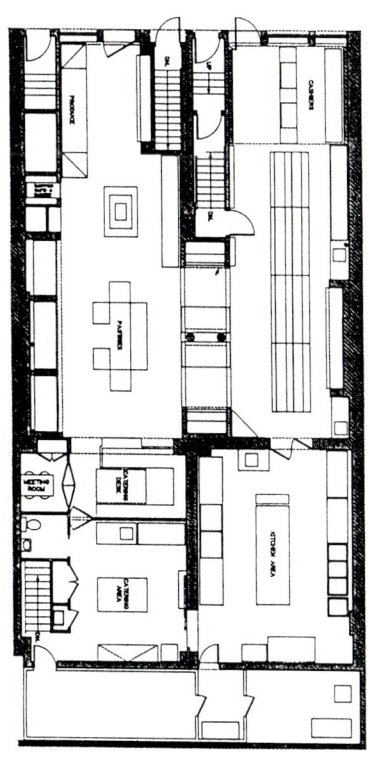

Design: Pentagram Design, New York, NY
Partner/Architect: James Biber
Partner/Graphics: Paula Scher
Arch. Assistant: Michael Zweck Bronner

KÄFER

Munich, Germany

When one speaks of the great food shops — of the gourmet food emporiums — around the world, certain names are sure to appear. One may speak of Fauchon's in Paris, of Harrod's Food Hall in London, Peck's in Milan, Ka De We in Berlin — and of Käfer in Munich.

Located in an historic building on Prinzregentenstrasse is Käfer. Five full floors are devoted to the presentation of gourmet foods and packaged products from all over the world as well as cafes and restaurants where one can sample the luscious wares in sumptuous settings. In addition, Käfer is also renowned for its catering service and they can provide for up to 2000 guests almost anywhere in the world. The gourmet shop also offers food and wine services at eight of Munich's opera houses and theaters.

Everywhere there is wood, tiles, marble and glints of brass and the sparkle of crystal. Whether it is in the produce department where Bavarian grown produce appears on display alongside exotic fruits and vegetables flown in for the discerning Käfer customer or in the Delicatessen area where the shopper can select from hundreds of meats, fishes, condiments, jams and jellies, and desserts, the presentation is always flawless. There are specialty food areas within the food emporium such as a meat department, a fresh daily fish and shellfish selection, and even a wine cellar that holds over a million bottles. The wine shop, like the other shops, is staffed by specialists who are knowledgeable and expert in the field; ready to suggest, advise or even select for the overwhelmed shopper. The bakery provides over 130 assorted freshly baked items or they will custom bake from the shopper's own recipe. The pastry shop is an experience all on its own!

The motto at Käfer is — "alles is möglich" — Anything is Possible. No matter what the shopper may want, his or her wish can be satisfied in this unique establishment which combines the comfort and convenience of the corner grocery store with the most exotic of gourmet palaces. One has only to ask.

KINTETSU DEPT. STORE MARKET
Nara, Japan

In the tradition of most Japanese department stores, the lower level of the retail establishment is devoted to a market with areas of prepared foods. The basement level one of the new Kintetsu store in Nara is the market shown here.

The super presentation of produce and prepared foods is set out over 44,000 sq. ft. The designers, Interspace Time, were particularly challenged because of the great variety of both Western and Japanese food counters that had to be accommodated along with the numerous food "vendor" shops — spaces rented by manufacturers or producers which are another part of the Japanese retail tradition.

IST established a theme palette of natural woods, stone, and light colors which they used extensively throughout much of the store. "It opened up each area of the market and also provided a fine background for the simple, but traditionally-styled, art deco detailing. American-style lighting was also introduced which "emphasized the feature merchandise yet gave character by combining a soft general lighting with a different array of accent lamps."

Colorful murals of shellfish and fish adorn the yellow/gold wall behind the "Daily Food Market" where fresh foods are available daily. Directly below is the Akishino Fuzei stand which is classically Japanese in design, and it is a "vendor" shop. The "Confectionery Counter," on the bottom of the opposite page, shows off Western-style cakes and pastries. The register of the Fresh Food area is shown above.

The total effect of the food hall is "an elegant and detailed image creating a strong aesthetic identity translating into a time honored classic."

Design: Interspace Time, Tokyo, Japan
Principal in Charge: Stome Usihidate
Vice President/Project Manager: Hiroyuki Kawano
Project Designer: Alex Soto
Design Coordinator: Yuka Mizutani
Kintetsu Coordinator: Goro Hashimoto
Photographer: Yasuhiro Gotoh

Harvey Nichols Market
Harvey Nichols Dept. Store, Knightsbridge, London, England

Knightsbridge in London is synonymous with class and elegance. Harvey Nichols, located in Knightsbridge — only three streets away from Harrod's — is an internationally-known fashion specialty store where designer clothes are beautifully presented in the boutique filled store. The "crowning" achievement at HN is this newly opened food market and gourmet shop on the top level of the specialty store with its own cafe/coffee shop which will be shown in the next chapter.

The central area of the fifth floor has been opened up to daylight with angled fabric shades that shield the shoppers but still allow the fruits and vegetables on display here to be seen as though in an open air market. The gray and white terrazzo floor is a checker board pattern — laid at an angle — to further "open" up the space.

The angled awnings above are yellow and white while the walls are also white and identified as The Fifth Floor is gray letters of a refined type. The produce is arranged in colorful compositions atop gray and white accented counters. A plethora of incandescent spots further enhance the warm, sunny ambience of this marketplace even when the traditional "foggy day" takes over in London town.

Store Operations Controller: John S. Kettle
Food & Beverage Director: Dominic Ford
Director of Display & Advertising: Mary Portas
Photographer: MMP/RVC

Beyond the produce area, in carefully lit and colorfully painted spaces with lowered ceilings, one finds the assorted packaged and prepared foods — all aglow under the incandescent lights. The high-tech, utilitarian, chromed metal shelving units that hold the tins and boxes create the aisles where overhead the ceiling is enlivened with colorful patterns of primary colored rectangles and signage to help the shopper find her way through the maze. There is a bakery where one can buy freshly baked breads, rolls and cakes and a coffee department where one can have blends created and ground to order. In addition there are meat stands, fish, cheese and deli counters for the shopper to peruse. Always there are the straw baskets brimming over with selections which add a warm and cozy touch to the HN market along with the wonderful displays on top of and in the counters.

This market has a look all its own. It doesn't attempt to be the classic English Food Hall or the charming French charcuterie. It does come off as a smart and stylish place to pick up a few things for a party — or even a meal — along with the clothes to wear when entertaining.

Rumpel

Heitzing, Vienna, Austria

Nasch Markt is in the heart of Vienna while Rumpel is located on the outskirts of Vienna — just a street or two from the entrance to the grounds and gardens of the Imperial Schoenbrun Palace. This is not a "gourmet" or "specialty" food shop, but a local store that caters to the middle class shoppers who live in this suburb.

The almost floor-to-ceiling windows are outlined with a rich, warm brown wood, the same wood that extensively lines most of the walls inside the compact market. The script "Rumpel," in red, is scrawled across the white fascia of the shopfront. Inside, all is white — and wood. The floor is laid with large white ceramic tiles and the dado and some of the counters are white laminate. The natural wood panelling lines the walls and the shelving is constructed of the same material. The refrigerated counters that hold the meats, cheeses, and prepared foods are finished in white, and they rest on wooden bases. A two foot wide fascia of mirror bridges the space between the wood veneered walls and the white plaster ceiling which is patterned with recessed incandescent spotlights. The warm light fills the store and balances the fluorescents that are used inside the refrigerated cases.

Hanging plants, counter top displays and special presentations of the fruits and vegetables and the freshly baked breads and rolls all "decorate" the simple, neutral setting and make this little "local" shop a stand-out in small market design.

Photographer: MMP/RVC

CHARCOUTIERE TRAITEUR
Chartres, France

Have you ever noticed how many people stop and press their noses to glass when the product that is displayed is food? People will oh! and ah!, drool and dribble over food, especially when the presentation is as exquisite as it is in some stores.

The Charcoutiere Traiteur is just an everyday, not very spectacular or special, food shop in Chartres. It is really for the "natives." But — the store has been designed with love and with respect for the merchandise and the customers. It starts with the beautifully-arranged trays of prepared foods in the window — on glass shelves and illuminated from above by flattering incandescent light. Inside the shop is an eclectic mix of rough, wood beamed ceilings, wood cabinetry, and natural baked ceramic tile floors. The contemporary refrigerated fixtures are black and glass and highlighted with brass accents. Old fashioned lantern lights hang from the rustic ceiling spreading warm light over the foods which are also illuminated from within the cases.

The walls of the shop are lined with shallow shelves and everything is within easy reach of the shopper.

Photographer: MMP/RVC

FLO PRESTIGE

Printemps Dept. Store, Paris, France

Photographer: MMP/RVC

For many, many years shoppers would find a quiet haven and a simple repast awaiting them under the fabulous stained glass dome atop the century old Printemps Department Store in Paris. In addition to this spacious "garden" which is now ringed with coffee bars and espresso shops, there is now a new, small but finely stocked gourmet shop, Flo Prestige, standing just before the entrance into the restaurant. The white interior sparkles in the bright light provided by the dropped, fluorescent illuminated ceiling and the sharp accenting spotlights.

In addition to the food square white ceramic tiles on the floor and the almost pristine white walls, most of the multiple leveled floor units are finished with a white laminate. The low ceiling of the space is covered with a reflective metal sheeting that adds to the kinetic energy of the shop. The various categories of food products available are noted in white and a black fascia that runs around the perimeter of the space. Since the signs are illuminated from behind, the lettering stands out from the sparkle and shine of the reflective ceiling.

It is the warm glowing incandescent light that tints the white walls and adds a peachy tone over some of the other stark white surfaces in this totally neutral setting. The deep mulberry color that appears in the logo design on the outside of the open-for-viewing shop is sparingly used on the interior for accent notes, on the packaging and on the graphics used on the selling floor.

TESSI
Chartres, France

Another small store that adds to the French crown of epicurean treats. Tourists do not usually shop Tessi; this store is for the locals only since it is not near any of the attractions that would generally attract tourists. The small corner store is truly a mom-and-pop operation. The sign outside proclaims "Patisserie" on one side and "Boulangerie" on the other; it is a bakery.

Inside the shop is almost square with windows on two sides but still it has a warm and cozy ambience about it. The ancient building that houses the shop is evident in the wood beam construction of the ceiling. The floor is laid with hexagonal shaped ceramic tiles in assorted shades of beige and the pastry counters are constructed of oak wood with applied panel details and angled glass fronts. The walls are also covered with matching wood shelves and through the openings one can see the rich terra cotta of the actual wall. The products on the shelves are illuminated by a fluorescent tube hidden behind the valance of the shelving unit.

Adding to the look and texture of the shop are the fluted milk glass pendant lights that hang down from the dark wood beamed ceiling. They add a warm ambient light to the natural colored materials used in the shop. The "user friendly" counter top displays also add to the charm and "color" of the shop.

Photographer: MMP/RVC

Maison Du Fromage
Chartres, France

Across the street from an old glass and iron, Art Nouveau, covered market is the Maison Du Fromage which not only offers a wide range of domestic and imported cheeses but also has the biscuits, crackers, wines and confiteurs to go with the cheeses. One window of the shop is filled with wine bottles and assorted jars of jellies and jams while the other features some prepared foods and also boasts of the French Pates within.

The interior is contemporary/rustic. It is a clean shop that in its design attempts to recall the provincial past. The wooden cases are not overly detailed and the timbered construction in the rear of the store and the supporting wood column do recall interiors like the Tessi which were actually built in old houses.

The floor is covered with squares of creamy marble and the walls are also a pale warm beige outlined and defined with natural wood moldings and shelves. Throughout the space is illuminated by incandescent spots and even the cheese-filled cases seem to glow with warm, flattering light. Artifacts and "antiques" are used to "decorate" the shop and add to the illusion of "tradition" and "heritage" which seems to be so important for the customers of this local cheese store.

Photographer: MMP/RVC

KELLEY & PING
Greene St., New York, NY

The architects/designers of Kelley & Ping ask us "to imagine a bustling sidewalk in the middle of Hong Kong — urban, dense, slightly industrial. Immediately off the street, a noodle shop/tea shop/grocery — meant to feel timeless and authentic." This is what the designers recreated in the tall ceilinged space of 2000 sq. ft. in an old building on Greene St. in the Soho district in New York City.

This exciting space combines old and new elements in surprisingly unexpected ways to create a shop that seems to be "woven with the threads of time." It seems as though it has always been there.

This combination grocery/restaurant is bright and airy for all of its atmosphere. Through the narrow windows, the shopper can see most of the 90' space even to the dining area in the rear where the 16' ceiling is pierced with skylights. This becomes the focal point in the store. Also visible is the wide array of teas, housewares and some tiny tables. The teas and grocery products are contained within beautiful wood cases which have a warm and rich look while "stark, unadorned light bulbs and a front wall left untreated, are startling, but feel contextual." It may have been many, many years since that front wall has been painted so the aged "patina" adds to the total ambience of the space. A clean, new counter, in contrast rests on a red floor "whose paint is already fading to green."

The design style and variety of materials are eclectic like the function of the space itself and very much like the cross section of its New York customers — or for that matter, the people of Hong Kong."

Design: L. Bogdanow, New York, NY
Design Team: Larry Bogdanow and Warren Ashworth

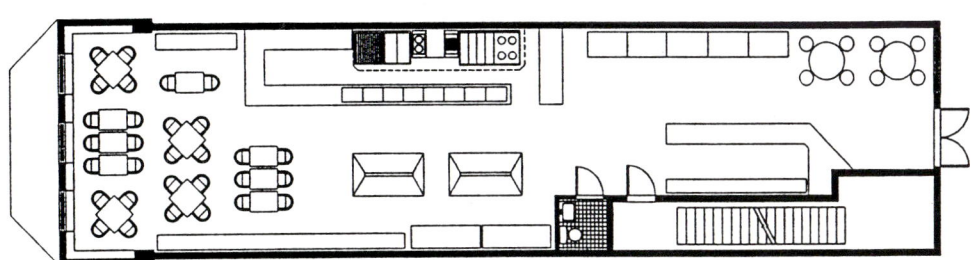

KNOTT'S BERRY MARKET
Mall of America, Bloomington, MN

Knott's Berry Market store makes a starring appearance in Snoopy's domain in the vast Mall of America. Here the happy shoppers can load up on a complete selection of world famous jams, jellies, and other food/gift products. The market is a rich, warm and woody place filled with sights, smells and hundreds of products appealingly displayed on easy-to-reach counters, shelves, and gondolas.

The space is flooded with warm incandescent light that reflects off the off-white walls and ceiling. Cracker barrels, pine tables, braided rugs, homespun fabrics, old pink bricks, bits and pieces of nostalgia — they are all collected to create "the nostalgic sights and smells of Mrs. Knott's own kitchen." To intrigue the shoppers, the floor layout is a maze of low wooden gondolas that allow the shoppers to get "lost" and "discover" worthwhile finds along the way out.

The visitor is invited to move along the smooth, oversized brick tile aisle where the supporting columns and feature walls are textured with faded, variegated bricks — all to further the "old fashioned, home goodness" of the products arranged under the fluorescent ceiling fixtures and highlighted by the accenting spots which are arranged to correspond to the floor fixture layout on the floor. Some merchandised areas are covered with a rich blue carpet as in the area where the "antique" leggy stove serves as a fixture; it becomes a prop along with the memorabilia collected on and around it.

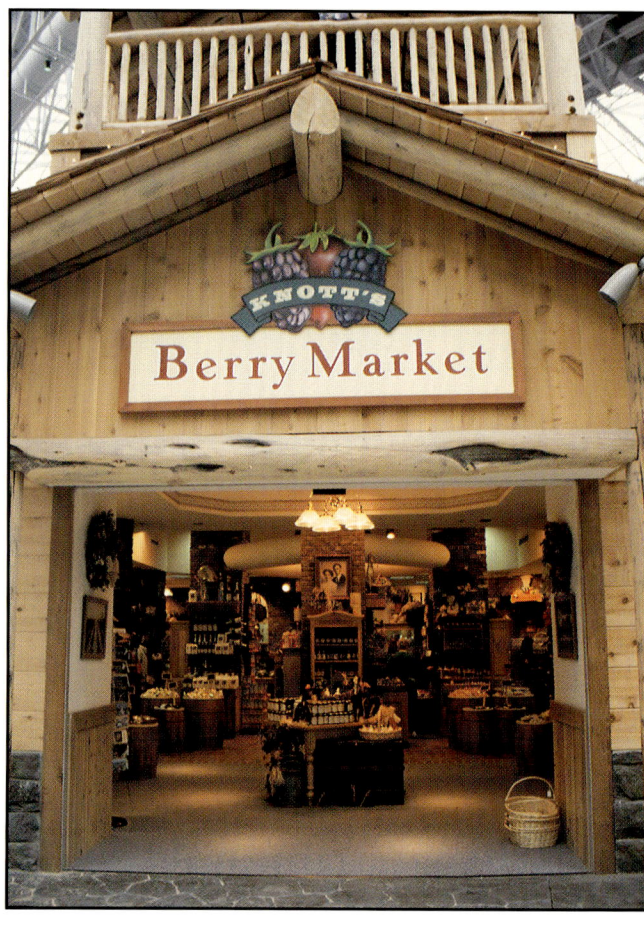

Photographer: MMP/RVC

As the country becomes more "gourmet-coffee" conscious, Knotts Berry Market is right on top of the trend with a free standing wall of wood and brass that stores and shows off a variety of blends ready for special grinding and packaging. Here, too, memorabilia and artifacts are used to further the store's image. For those who can't wait to taste the coffee they have purchased, there is a coffee/espresso bar where shoppers can relax and watch peanut butter being made or see the fudge being stretched and kneaded on large marble tables.

There is something wholesome and fresh about this market in which a romantic, story-book way brings nostalgia into the retail scene.

LOEB'S BAKERY
Loeb Supermarket, Ottawa, Ontario, Canada

Loeb Supermarkets appear throughout Canada and they have been successful in promoting an image of a store where things are fresh and "just picked." The bakery area has recently been redesigned by Dorf Associates of New York and the prototype, shown here, attempts to set forth the new "fresh baked from scratch" look which will hopefully maximize sales.

In addition to the aroma that arises from the preparation area and the bakery ovens which are in full view of the shoppers, the designers have emphasized the "abundance" of the fresh breads with displays that seem to tumble and overflow with products that all but reach out and say "take me." The device that succeeds here is that the breads and other baked goods are set out in a variety of heights — at different eye levels — in an assortment of "homey" and "country style" woven reed baskets accented with homespun, rustic-style napkins. The shopper can almost touch the merchandise but a light, almost invisible marble topped counter does separate the shopper from the merchandise. The counter bases, the shelves and provincial units along the wall with a fascia that arcs forward and up are all constructed of stained maple. They add to the "hearth and home" ambience that reinforces the wholesale quality of the baked goods.

Design: Dorf Associates, New York, NY
Martin Dorf

Custom graphics and the arch motif that spans over the sign board also contribute to the new look. Though the bakery is part of a full supermarket, the designers have created a specialty store look which is enhanced by the incandescent lighting plan which also furthers the "image of quality."

Pasadena Baking Company
Pasadena, CA

Design: Akar, Santa Monica, CA
Design Team: Sat Garg, Michelle Gill, Bedros Bedros
Photographer: John Post

This French/Italian bakery is situated next to Mi Piace, also designed by Akar for the same owners in the historic Exchange Bldg. in the old town district of downtown Pasadena. The companion cafe/espresso bar is located further on in this book.

Based on bakeries in Paris, the designer, Sat Garg, found that what makes them such a vital part of the culture is the close relationship between the working bakery and the retail space. At the Pasadena Baking Company, a large opening connects the retail area and the working bakery — exposing the impressive stainless steel ovens. This way the customer can enjoy the sight, scent and the sounds of the bread making process — "guaranteeing active sensory participation."

For the retail space the design firm came up with a textural and contemporary environment composed of rectangular abstract forms and clean lines, and materials like limestone for the floors and birds-eye maple cabinetry and cases — to bring warmth and richness to the bakery. Everything was custom designed by Akar even the unique bases for the small cafe tables in the coffee shop part of the bakery. The bakery ovens and glass display cases were provided by Guyon of France.

Sat Garg fulfilled his promise to the client and did provide a "visual delight."

Design: 61st Place Architects, Scottsdale
Photographer: Dan Watts

BOULDERS BAKERY / CAFE

El Pedregal, The Boulders, Scottsdale, AZ

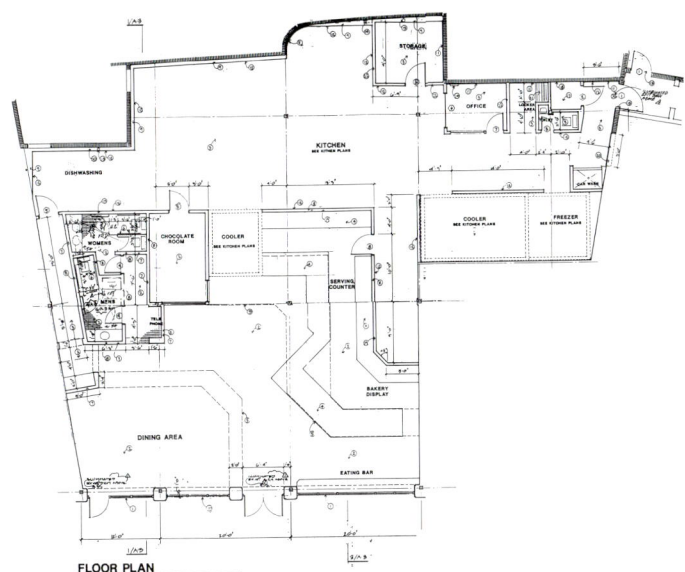
FLOOR PLAN

El Pedregal, on the outskirts of fashionable Scottsdale, is a mall with a difference. In addition to its unique architecture and coloration, it is truly a "festival place" all year round. The architects of El Pedregal also designed the Boulders Bakery/Cafe as a casual indoor/outdoor type of shop that specializes in baked goods, coffee and tea.

To play up the earthy, Southwestern look of the center and its location, there is a baked ceramic tile floor, a coffered ceiling with moving fans, rattan chairs and tables inlaid with patterns of tiles to further enhance the decorative scheme. There are display cases which feature the baked goods, breads and pastries at the sales counter and the espresso machine, coffee mills and brewers, and tea pots are all placed in full view of the patrons on the rear counter. The designers have used the same color palette and geometric motifs that they used to adorn the El Pedregal center and so this warm, sand-beige interior is accented with aquas, teals, pinks, and corals.

Chocolate Chariot

The Forum, Las Vegas, NV

Shortly after this candy store was opened in the new Forum shopping center in Las Vegas it had to be "re-decorated" because it somehow did not quite go with the classically-inspired theme of The Forum. Leslie Parraguerre of Colours, Inc. was called upon to "romanticize" the store; to do a creative cosmetic job on what was there.

The designer selected a glowing peach/beige color of polymix paint which was applied over the existing plastic laminate casework and the moldings. The concrete floor was etched, stained and stenciled with "Roman" motifs and then sprinkled with colored mosaic glass to "age" it — and also to further tie the shop in with the look of the center just beyond the doors. Merchandise is displayed on the color washed floor on assorted size "classic" pedestals and columns which are also treated with the peach-toned polymix paint or antiqued in off-white.

The store is illuminated by incandescent spots which are recessed within the dropped, acoustical ceiling of the store.

Design: Colours, Inc., Las Vegas, NV

Confetti Chocolat
Embarcadero, San Francisco, CA

This 850 sq. ft. shop is located on the street level of the Embarcadero Center Four in San Francisco and it was conceived as both a chocolate/candy shop and a coffee store/bar. We have set it here at the end of this chapter along with the bakery/cafes on the previous pages to serve as a segue into the next chapter which deals with the growing interest and popularity of coffee and tea shops and bars across this country and in other places — and how architects and designers are treating the'm.

To create a visual identity for the small spaces, the designers added curved elements into the design which also help to create a traffic pattern in the dual operation. The sweeping arcs that are the coffee bar and the candy counter are covered with cherry wood veneer while the table tops in the seating area are made of birch; some are finished in natural birch and some are stained the color of the cherry wood and all are accented with black. The designers worked with the existing concrete floor which they had stained and scored into a giant diamond pattern — angled to visually stretch the space. The floor is finished in terra cotta, ocher and blue/green. The cool color is also used for the neon that lights up the circular cut-out in the ceiling and neon strips also appear beneath the cherry wood counters making them "float" in the space. The lighting for this shop is mainly from the recessed incandescent spots and the accenting low voltage lamps.

Design: Ohashi Design, San Francisco, CA
Alan & Joy Ohashi

LCBO Mini-Shop
First Canadian Place, Toronto, Ontario, Canada

The Liquor Control Board of Ontario, the government run operation, desired a new "mini-store image with an up market, fast track approach to retailing." The International Design Group of Toronto that has designed several of their other retail outlets was commissioned to design this store which would carry a complete line of wines and spirits.

The designers took an "arcade" approach to laying out the space in an attempt to allow for a "friendly and direct shopping experience" for the shopper. The simple and direct plan makes the store easy to access and assists the shopper in his or her orientation in the space. The "arcade" was created by adding new feature columns to match the existing white marble faced ones on the floor. Bright copper tubes with signage arch between the columns to join them together in a series of archways or arcades.

Elegant and rich materials were used throughout the store. The wall and floor fixtures combine burled elm and natural oak with accent bronze inlays. Polished and unpolished cream tiles are laid on the floor and patterned in geometric motifs with terra cotta and black tiles. The ambience is warm and friendly since the general illumination is provided by the incandescent lamps recessed into the ceiling beyond the glittering copper arches and low voltage lighting is used for the accent lighting throughout.

Design: International Design Group, Toronto, Ontario, Canada
Photographer: Design Archives

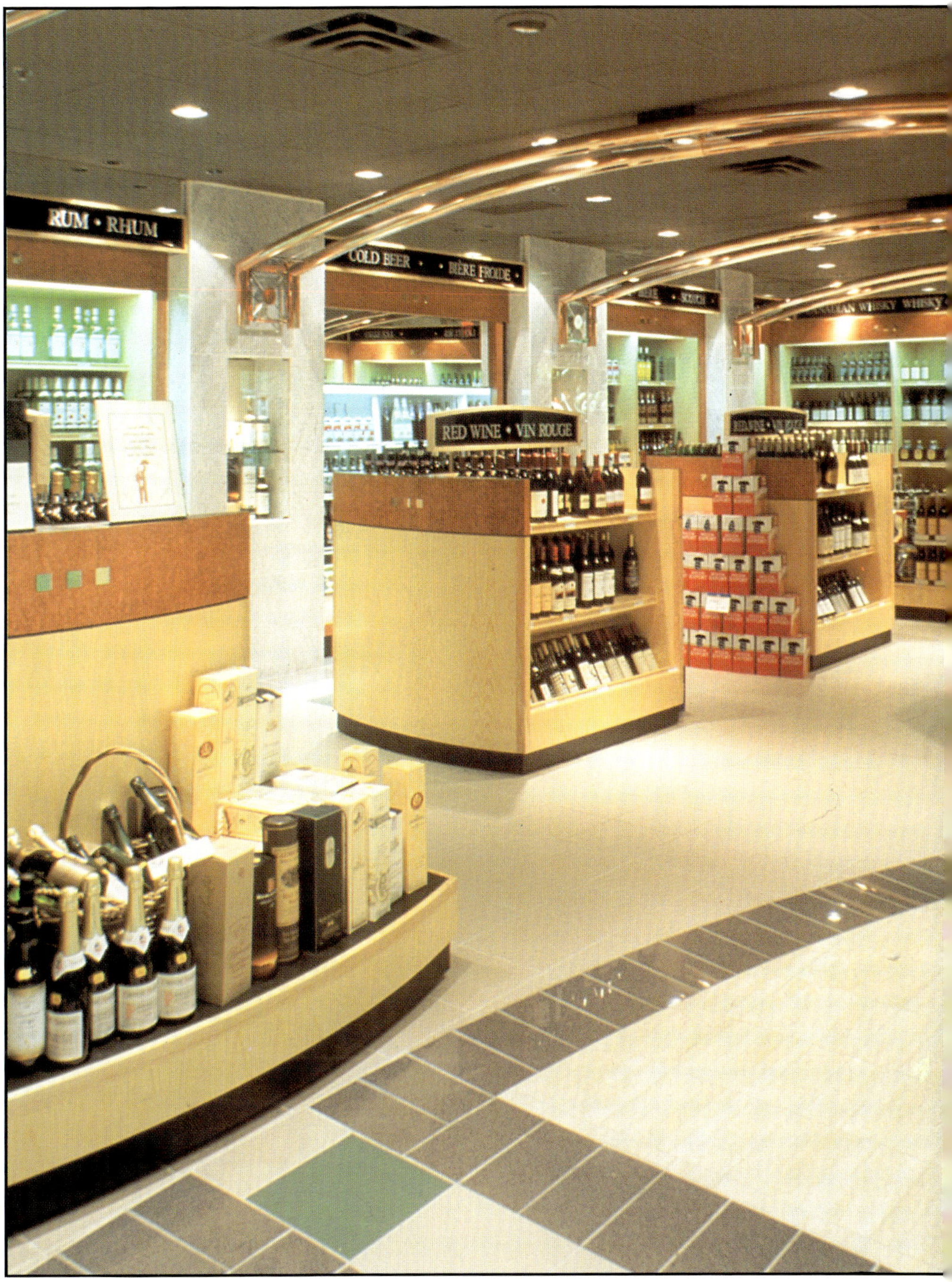
RUM • RHUM
COLD BEER • BIÈRE FROIDE
RED WINE • VIN ROUGE

VINS FINS
WHITE WINE • VIN BLANC

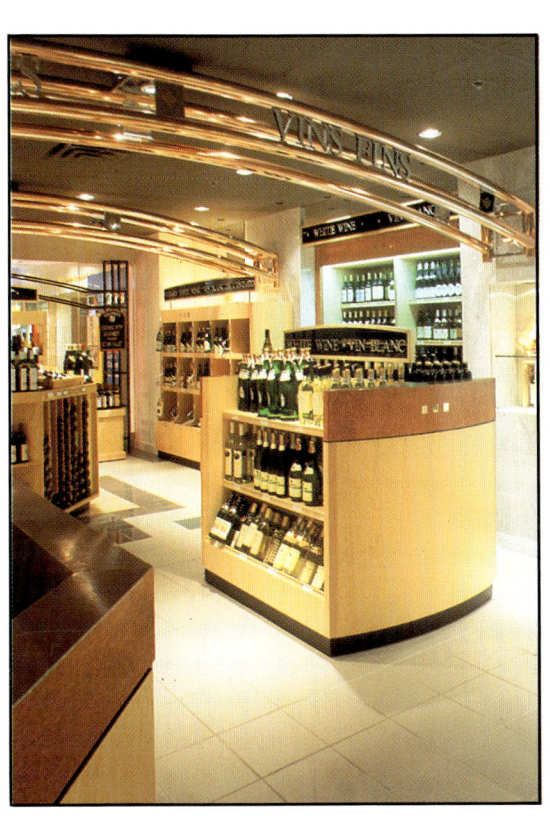

Coffee Bars, Coffee Shops, Coffee Stores & Cafes

Pasqua Coffee Bars
New York, Los Angeles, San Francisco

PASQUA COFFEE BARS
New York, Los Angeles, San Francisco

"Coffee is a social medium — a vehicle that has brought people together throughout the ages for the exchange of ideas," said Mark Zuckerman who along with Martin Kupferman founded this chain of coffee bars that now appear on both coasts. It was a Turkish servant to an English merchant, Pasqua Rosee, who way back in 1652 introduced the brew to London and in his honor the Pasqua name was adopted. To create the retail setting and also to supervise the graphics for the chain, Stephen Elbert of Elbert Associates of Oakland was selected.

The 31 Pasqua bars appeal to the "working" population and thus the sites selected are usually located near work or transit centers. Though the shops vary in size from a mere 50 sq. ft. up to 1300 sq. ft., the average space is about 500 sq. ft. From the original stand-up, coffee bars, the operation has expanded and now also serves baked goods, salads and paninis and there is limited seating in some of the larger units. According to the architect, Stephen Elbert, "as Pasqua became a full service food and beverage company, that presented new needs in terms of storage and displays for salads and sandwiches."

"The design direction has been corporate, yet whimsical and spontaneous." In each of the Pasqua sites, the store's design and architecture — though distinctive and individualistic — is still flexible enough to work with the architecture that surrounds it. Since the spaces and locations vary, so do the stores in design and thus there is no "cookie-cutter" format or roll-out program even though there are "signature" notes which do make the Pasqua Coffee Bar identifiable. One of these is the copper veneered bar and bar front that is the focal point of each shop. In addition, stone work is usually incorporated into the design along with tiled floors.

Design: Elbert Associates, Oakland, CA
  Steven Elbert
Photographers: N.Y. Sites: William Miller
  L.A. Sites: Sandra Williams
  S.F. Sites: Eric Sahlin

The recognizable store logo is prominently displayed both inside and outside the shop. The trapezoidal shape, in one variation or another, is also part of the store's design language. It may appear as fins dropped from the ceiling — parallel to the ground or perpendicular to it, as appliques are in the layout of the space. The same menu, cups and saucers, napkins and other service materials are used in each shop to continue the Pasqua "look."

According to Mark Zuckerman, "The stores are sufficiently similar to make them identifiable — but individual enough to capture visual interest."

On the opposite page:
Top: 200 Pine St., San Francisco, CA
Bottom: World Finance Center, New York, NY
On this page: Liberty Plaza, New York, NY
Bottom: 400 So. Hope, Los Angeles, CA
On the previous page: Century Tower, Los Angeles, CA

SEATTLE COFFEE ROASTERS
Fifth Ave., New York, NY

The new company decided to capitalize on the growing trend towards "fancy, Seattle-style coffee bars" — while still setting itself apart by providing the highest quality coffee drinks in a unique and stylish setting on what was once the "Ladies Mile" in fashionable old New York. In addition, the design firm, Adams, Rosenberg Kolb was called upon to develop an overall graphic identity for the company as well as the "interior design language that represents the client's philosophy" and that could be adapted to a variety of sites in the future.

The designers selected materials that contrast "natural richness with hard, industrial durability." Medite II paneling was finished with a warm Q.T. stain and it serves as a backdrop for the cooler metal and granite surfaces of the service counter. The counter is clad with a steel sheet metal fascia, acid etched to a pewter color, and it is bordered top and bottom with a four inch gunmetal finished steel band. A thin layer of Indian black absolute granite tops the gently curved counter and that sweep is replayed in the curving light valance above. This light valance is made of steel tubular trusses with 1/4" rod struts finished in the gunmetal, and it supports a 3" band of perforated steel with lumasite backing.

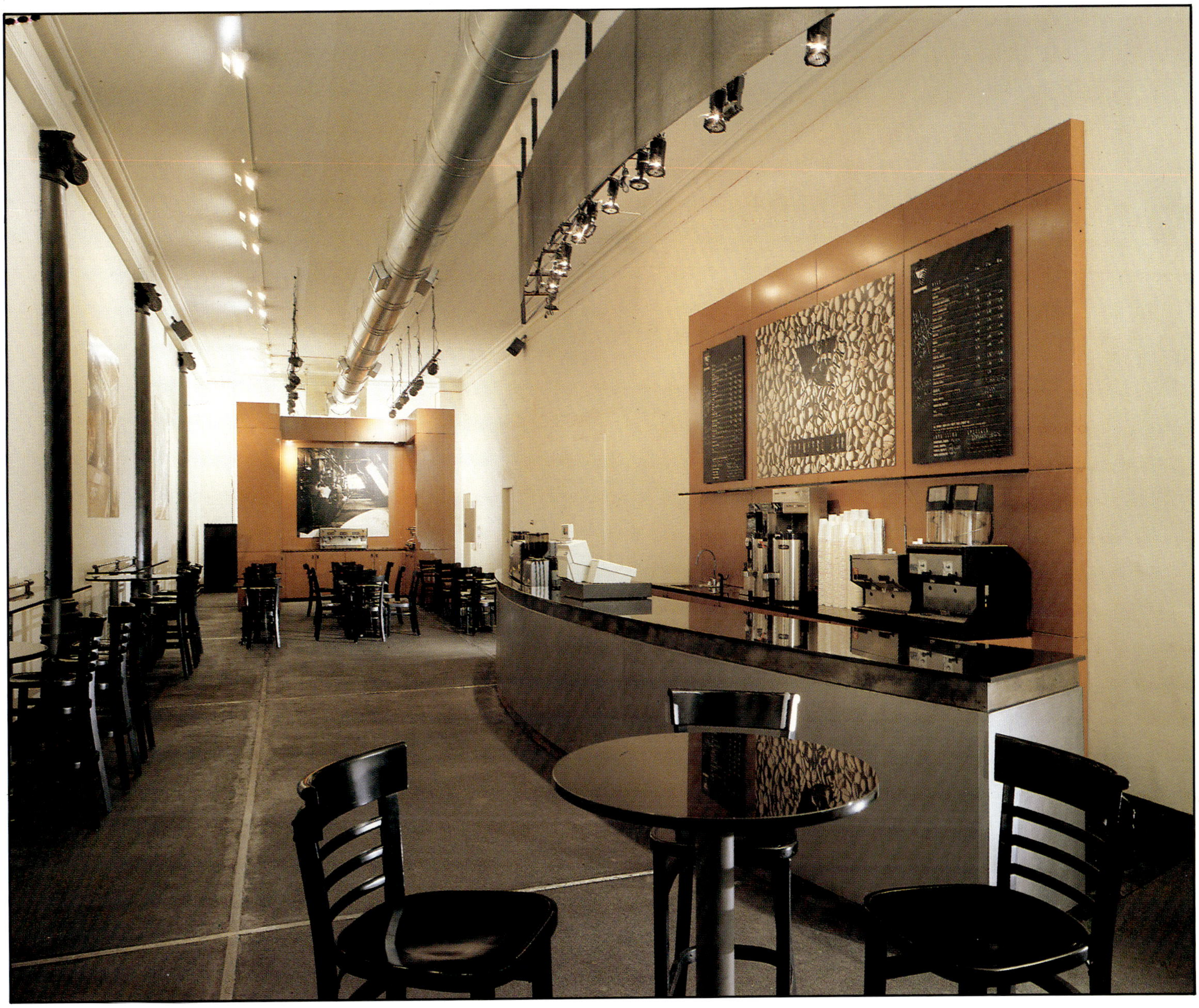

Design: Adams Rosenberg Kolb, New York, NY

The ceiling-hung valance carries clamp-on theatrical light fixtures which illuminate the back bar and counter top. T-bulbs provide a warm glow through the translucent fascia while hidden fluorescent fixtures, concealed over the duct, wash the ceiling.

The off-white Zolatone-finished space, with its 17 ft. high cast iron columns is decorated with enlarged sepia toned photographs of historic coffee scenes. A series of custom designed standing counters are also centered between the columns and the storefront. The counters are long, thin granite slabs supported by sandblasted steel posts which are bolted to the floor. A gunmetal foot-rest and a glass tube cup-rail filled with coffee beans, finish off the counters.

The 12 ft. high, movable display wall clad with the Medite II paneling stands in the rear of the seating area and it is supported on a steel frame with heavy duty casters so that the wall can be moved back and forth or even pivoted depending upon the needs of the moment.

Seattle Coffee Roasters has proven to be a great "in" coffee spot in the shadow of the historic Flat-Iron building. It caters to the advertising and fashion people who are taking over this lower end of Fifth Avenue.

NEW WORLD COFFEE
New York, NY

This coffee shop/bar was created to introduce "a new world of superior, darker roasted, more flavorful coffees and espresso beverages to New York City." The owners requested that the designer, Ronnette Riley, provide an ambience that echoes the "warmth of experience and aroma associated with authentic espresso beverages."

To establish the feeling, earth-tone ores, stone and wood were used along with a green/bold backdrop which contrasted with the cream colored walls and floor. Since the space is so small, the back wall of the space is highlighted so that the entire shop becomes the "storefront."

"The diagonal line was the prime motivator behind the scheme on both an experimental and a functional level." The counter with the pendant lights outlining it draws the eye into the space. "It works as a promotional device spurring a dialogue between the passerby and the shop. Its diagonal placement maintains a visual interaction with the outside — imposing an inviting impression for impromptu or future visits." By designing the counter on the hypotenuse, it maximizes its length and creates a deeper free space for activity in front and avoids the typical "galley" layout.

For the company's graphics, the designers sought to create "an icon that would accommodate and even evoke traditional rituals, pleasures and images associated with coffee drinking without resorting to stylized nostalgia." The logo design is a globe rising from the surrounding triangle's horizontal base in a copper glow surrounded by "rays" of steam. The idea of coffee is further suggested through the use of the earthy coffee colors in the logo's other applications. The typeface, Charlemagne, hints at the timeless tradition — like that of cultivating and drinking coffee.

Design: Ronnette Riley Architect, New York, NY
Architectural Team: Ronnette Riley, A.I.A., Principal
Dale Linden Turner, Project Arch.
Franco Ravennati, Assistant
Graphics Team: Ronnette Riley and Margot Perman
Photographer: Otto Baitz, Freehold, NJ

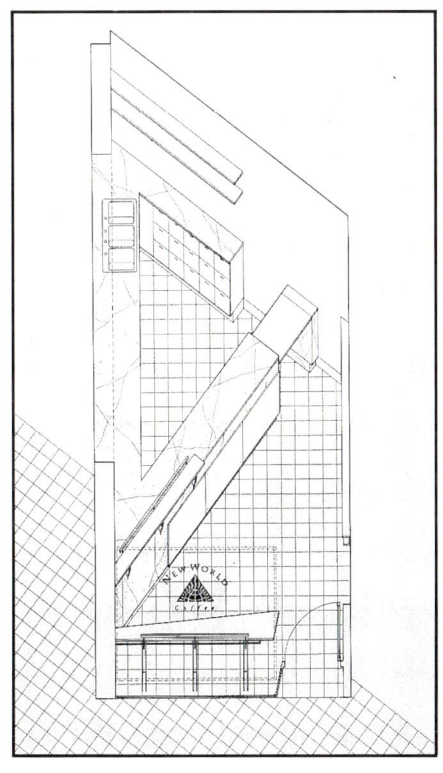

AROMAZ COFFEE AND PASTRY BAR

Harbor Place, Vancouver, BC, Canada

The project, as presented to Sunderland Innerspace Design, Inc. was to convert the 732 sq. ft. space that was once a custom service banking center into an exciting coffee and pastry bar. They were not to change the "existing architectural vocabulary" of the space and they also had to respect the existing ceiling heights and the spaces relationship to the World Trade Center lobby.

In answer to all the above, the designers conceived a setting which communicated its purpose to the street traffic by dynamic shapes, rich colors, distinct graphics and dramatic lighting effects. They took advantage of the high volume space by suspending a distinctive design element which helps to make the space seem more intimate yet it does not disrupt the existing ceiling lines.

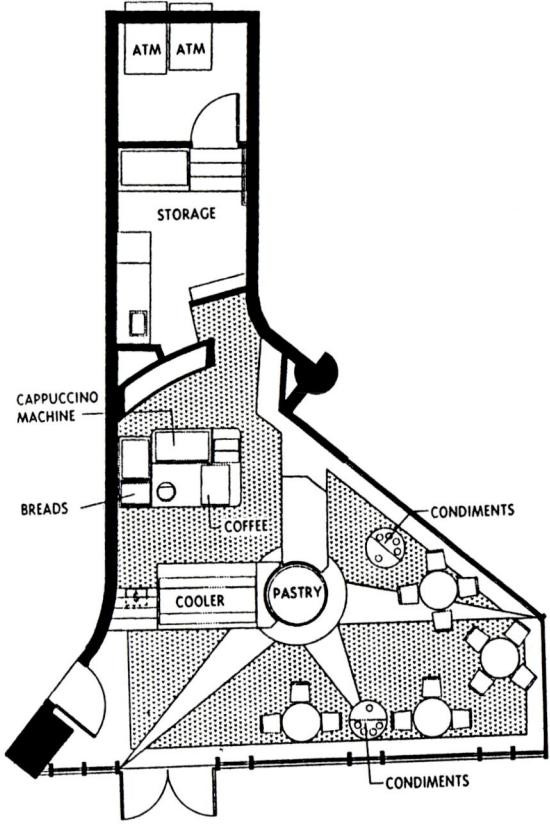

Design: Sunderland Innerspace Design, Inc., Vancouver, BC
Principal: Jon P. Sunderland, B.a.a., I.D., R.I.D.
Senior Designer: Scott Andrews, B.I.D.
Photographer: Melnychuk Photography

The unit reminds one of a coffee cup. The conical shape motif started with the suspended element and continued in the design as the rounded features on the pastry case and the custom table design and the support legs for the pastry bar. "The cones being reminiscent of the drip coffee process."

An entertaining and whimsical quality has also been incorporated into the design with the custom high chair design, the floor patterning motif and the hot, steaming coffee design on the exterior glass and on the suspended cone — that started it all. The design firm carefully coordinated their graphics with the work of the graphic design consultant on the job.

Barnie's

Barnies is one of the oldest and largest of the specialty gourmet coffee and tea companies that are rapidly rising and spreading across the country. Currently, Barnies has well over 80 stores in more than 16 states and the stores feature as many as 50 blends of coffee, espresso and/or cappuccino as well as 100 varieties of tea. In addition, the familiar mall landmark is filled with coffee and tea related products.

The look of Barnies starts with the architectural concept that was originally created by the founder of the company, B. Philip Jones, back in 1980. Since then it has undergone a series of revisions and up-dates but the store is still recognized by the hunter green exterior with gold details and trim, the green canvas awnings and the classically-inspired pedimented door and pilasters. Inside, the walls are usually creamy beige to complement the deep green flooring and the oak fixturing and shelving.

The green and white color scheme has been carried over to the paper cups, napkins, bags, boxes, brochures and signage used in the Barnies operation along with the Barnies name that appears on the store windows and on the awnings. As new products are introduced and new packaging is created, they are also related to the original graphic concept and designed to complement the interior trim and co-exist with the store's other packaging and signs. In maintaining this "graphic control," Jamie Utendorf, V.P. of Merchandising and Advertising for Barnies, knows that the shoppers recognize the Barnies value and tradition no matter in which Barnies outlet she shops.

The stylized quarter round awning in hunter green with the sloped bottom and the Barnies name in gold appears outside the store as well as on the store's printed materials and stationery.

Design Concept: B. Philip Jones, CEO of Barnies
Graphic Designs: Jamie Utendorf, V.P. of Marketing & Merchandising
& Staff

Barnie's Kiosks & Carts

Shown here are two of the free-standing coffee bar kiosks and carts designed for Barnies Coffee Stores. They are beginning to appear in malls and in other public spaces where people are ready all day long for a "coffee break."

The Barnies kiosk is designed so that people can be served from all four sides and it is even equipped with some stools so that a shopper can enjoy that "break" off her feet while sipping freshly-brewed coffee, cappuccino, espresso, or even a coffee cooler.

The hunter green, gold, and cream color scheme is carried through for immediate identity and some of the architectural signature details — like the fluted pilasters, are also incorporated. Note the Barnies logo — the half round awning with the scalloped bottom — also is prominently displayed on the kiosk.

Barnies Express Cart is topped with the familiar green canvas awning with half rounds at either end that extend out way beyond the cart itself. An auxiliary unit can be added where there is space. The cart and the kiosk provide not only the coffee and espresso drinks but also some baked selections. To buy the famous assortment of blends and grinds and to select from the numerous teas, the shopper has to find the fully equipped Barnies Coffee Store in the nearest mall.

Design: Schafer Associates, Oakbrook Terrace, IL

JAVA EXPRESS

With space being limited and the demand for instant gratification growing, the coffee cart has developed from the metal cart that was rolled through the office space to furniture-like units as sophisticated and attractive as this wood sheathed cart designed by Schafer Associates for Java Express.

The design has an early 20th century, pre-W.W. 1-Viennese look that is at once elegant, smart and suggestive of the graciousness associated with coffee drinking in European coffee bars rather than the quick, out-of-the-paper-cup one usually thinks of as a "coffee break." These carts not only have the selection of assorted kinds of coffees and teas, but they also carry some baked goods that "go with."

The curved black top of the cart is etched by the low flattened curve at the base. In addition to the rich, golden toned wood veneered surfaces of the cart, there is the matte finished black used to accent the wood as well as the low sheen of copper bands.

Heavy duty casters not only keep the body of the cart off the ground but also make it movable. The lower part of the unit has storage space for coffee, paper goods, and additional baked goods. These carts are scheduled to appear in malls, in office buildings and in public spaces to provide a "civilized" coffee break in a harried and hurried world.

The reader may also want to refer back to the kiosks shown in the coverage of Pasqua in this chapter.

HEISSEBERGER COFFEE & TEA

Haas Haus, Vienna, Austria

Coffee houses and Vienna are almost synonymous though this exquisite contemporary coffee and tea shop/bar is far from what one usually expects to find in the waltzy "old Vienna." This is the new expression and it is located in the most unique and outstanding contemporary structure in the midst of Vienna's historic and fine shopping area.

The Haas Haus was designed by Prof. Hans Hollhein and with its many unusual facade materials and treatments, its reflective surfaces, its juxtapositioning of forms and shapes, it contrasts with the old St. Stephan's Cathedral that is reflected in its facade and the 18th and 19th century buildings along the Graben.

Heisseberger's Coffee & Tea Shop is located on the street level of this five story, inner-city, vertical mall and multi-purpose building. The store's design complements its handsome modern marble and steel setting.

The space is sleek, sharp and clearly defined in black and white with accents of stainless steel, brass and some dark mahogany wood. One wall is almost completely covered with coffee beans and blends in matte stainless steel cannisters with window openings and nozzles for filling orders. The opposite wall contains a multitude of black and gold tea cannisters lined up on shelves that cross the store. There is a wall of windows that allows the shoppers on the street to look into the shop with its creamy travertine floor and black mirrored fascias as well as a display of the complementary accessories to coffee and tea drinking. From the mall, there is also a wall of glass as well as the door into the shop. In addition to the black fronted counters with the white laminate tops, there are some stand-up tables and counters where the immediate need for a coffee fix can be satisfied. Here we see the introduction of the wood surfaces. The space is warmly illuminated by the low voltage spots recessed into the ceiling.

Photographer: MMP/RVC

L'Epicure

Ile St. Louis, Paris, France

Anybody who has ever wandered about in Paris — on the Left or Right Bank — must have at one time slowed down to enjoy the relaxed and tasteful shopping on the long but narrow Ile St. Louis which lies between the two banks of the Seine. On the long shopping street that forms the spine of the island is L'Epicure — a delicious shop that specializes in coffee, tea, chocolate, and preserves.

The exterior facade is part of the venerable building that houses the store and it is painted a rich, deep green. The logo, in gold, appears on the fascia over the door. Inside, the small and compact store is almost totally sheathed in a tawny, mellow colored wood.

The floor is covered with small, off-white ceramic squares and the area over the high wood library wall cabinets is painted a subtly muted terra cotta color. Logos and old time advertisements for coffee, tea, and chocolate products are framed and create a decorative band around the store — over the merchandise.

The wall shelves gently step back — the deepest shelf being the lowest one — so that the merchandise on the upper shelves can be seen and reached. In the center of the store are some rustic tables covered with gift suggestions and pre-wrapped gifts. The cash/wrap desk stands directly behind them and thus an island of merchandise in the center creates the traffic pattern.

NEWSBAR
W. 19th St., New York, NY

Design: Turett Collaborative Architects, New York, NY
Designer: Wayne Turett
Design Team: Norine Williams, Lester Tour, Bruce Garmendia
Graphic Design: Tracy Turner Designs
Photographer: Paul Warchol, New York, NY

The old, old fashioned coffee houses where people sat for hours reading newspapers or periodicals while sipping from a cup of coffee has been re-interpreted for today by Wayne Turett of Turett Collaborative Architects of New York. In a 600 sq. ft., stripped down space, the designer has combined magazines devoted to art, photography, fashion, theatre, and such, with a coffee bar that serves espresso, cappuccino, desserts and sandwiches.

As the passerby on W. 19th St. walks down between Fifth and Sixth Aves., he or she sees the entire operation on view through the floor to ceiling panes of glass. In keeping with the architect's belief that "the simpler — the better," he omits decoration and ornamentation from this space with its 16 ft. ceilings. Like the sidewalk outside, the floor within is concrete only warmer in color. The concrete topped counter rests atop a base constructed of stainless steel, galvanized metal and fiberglass panels. Though there is seating for only 12, there is room to accommodate "standees." There are "satellite" tables with aluminum tops and steel pipe bases that have metal seats attached to them that revolve around the fixed central element.

According to the designer, "the use of raw materials is kind of a subtle play. The more you place in there, the more it dilutes the effect and the rawness of the design is so effective when set against the refined qualities of the espresso machine and the magazines. The industrial components and elements help counter the expectation that people often have to coffee bars and newsstands."

The magazines are lined up on galvanized metal and brushed steel shelf racks which are placed against one of the plaster finished walls. The shelves can swing out and away from the wall, thus adding a sense of action and dynamics to the space. The TV monitors set over the coffee counter also add to the "news coverage" of the magazine shop.

The store's graphics are by Tracy Turner Design, and they include the logo design of the coffee cup with the wave-like lines rising from the cup as well as the type for Newsbar. The space is warmly lit by industrial stonco lamps and by track lights up on the ceiling that accentuate the magazines and the menu items.

KA DE WE CAFES ON THE SIXTH FLOOR

Ka De We Dept. Store, Berlin, Germany

This almost century-old department store stands in the heart of what was once West Berlin's major shopping area. One didn't just go to KaDeWe to shop — but "to see and be seen." Today, with the newly renovated Sixth and Seventh floors of the building — with the expanded food market and the effective, light-filled atrium, the coffee shops and cafes that ring this atrium on the Sixth floor have become the new place to "see and be seen." As the reader will find in the next chapter, there are other food operations available to the KaDeWe shopper in the stunning new Wintergarten on the seventh level.

The stands shown here are actually part of the gourmet food floor where epicures from Germany and other parts of the world can find the special and the unique. Like the food hall at Harrod's, it has a world-wide reputation and the 5800 sq. meter space makes it the largest food department in Europe with 600 employees of whom 100 are chefs and confectioners.

The individual cafes/food shops around the atrium are identified by their graphics and individual signage and detailing; from seafood specialties — to native staples to the more exotic. Each shop, though individual in look and design, seems to blend together in the black and white plus wood color palette which is accentuated with touches of color and sparkling brass. The white tiled floor is sometimes repeated on the rear wall of a stand — maybe in a smaller scale. Each unit is warmly illuminated either by spots recessed into the ceiling or by special pendant fixtures over the food offerings. Adding to the quality of the whole space is the presentation of the foods in glass fronted containers and the white toqued chef performing their magic in the open to viewing galleys that are part of the narrow food bars.

Design: Ernsting & Parlner
Photographer: MMP/RVC

Harvey Nichols - Fifth Floor
Harvey Nichols, Knightsbridge, London

Much more casual, indeed, is the coffee shop in the new Harvey Nichols market (see the previous chapter). Here the coffee shop is located at one end of the open, sky-lit produce area with a view of Brompton Rd. and London beyond the floor to ceiling windows. The wood topped tables have spindly black, criss-crossed legs and the donut-backed chairs are gaily finished in the golden yellow and bright blue that appear in the graphics throughout the market. Along one wall is a stainless steel and gray service counter where the coffee and tea is poured and also the salads, sandwiches and soups are prepared and from where one gets the freshly baked desserts. The gray and white terrazzo floor with the diagonally-oriented checkerboard design blends with the gray of the service counter.

Photographer: MMP/RVC

In a separate area is the Coffee and Tea stand where a wide assortment of coffee beans and blends can be selected from the glass and brass containers lined up along the rear wall of the open space. Up front is a sweeping black lacquered, wood-topped counter that also serves as a coffee bar for those who don't want to sit down to be served in the cafe in the produce area. The stand is also equipped with machines that grind the beans to the customer's order. Spotlights on tracks drop down from the ceiling to light up the space.

Deutsches Museum Cafe
Munich, Germany

The Mathias Thoerner Design firm was commissioned to design three distinct dining facilities in the Deutsches Museum in Munich, and here we present the cafe which can accommodate up to 90 persons. In the following chapter we will discuss the Snack Bar/Cafeteria which was designed to accommodate 60 persons.

Management demanded "strong color and formal language which would not only represent the 'zeitgeist' (spirit or essence) of the times but would also evoke the purpose and history of the museum." The design team took its inspiration from the "machine-age posters" of the 1920s and they relied on primary colors to achieve their goal. Yellow was used — bright and sunny — for the cafe which is located in one of the museum's towers with a wonderful view of Munich that stretches out to the Alps. As the reader will note, red was the color selected for the snack bar and a meditative and soothing blue accents the restaurant area.

Since the cafe is more intimate and personal than the Snack Bar, single chairs are pulled up to the smaller scaled tables. The table tops and counter tops in the cafe are made of gray/green terrazzo with the counters laminated with sandblasted stainless steel.

The wall lamps enhance "the rhythm of the windows as a given architectural component of the space" while the ceiling overhead is patterned with recessed low voltage lamps. Lighting fixtures, custom designed by Mathias Thoerner, were used throughout including the long pendant tube drops over the serving counter.

Design: Mathias Thoerner Design, NY

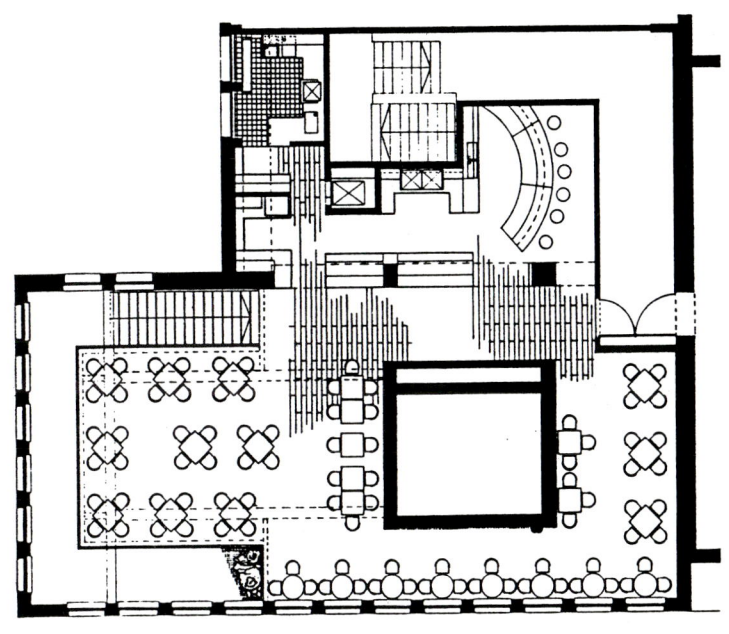

Hundertwasser Museum Cafe
Vienna, Austria

One of the truly unique treasures amid the many treasures to be found in Vienna is the Hundertwasser Museum tucked away in a residential part of the city — away from the busy, tourist part of Vienna. Designed by the architect/artist/philosopher and political activist, Hundertwasser, the museum is situated inside of a unique building covered with various geometric patterns of black and white tiles — full of irregular shapes and forms, curving and flowing lines and trees growing out of oddly-located windows. It is a "house that does not correspond to the usual cliches and norms — it is an adventure of modern times — a journey into the land of creative architecture, a melody for the feet and the eyes."

One of the more enchanting areas of the museum is the coffee shop/cafe on the main level which is entered through a handsome and unusual door from the main lobby of the museum. The cafe ambles out and away from the enclosing structure out into the garden beyond which is partially contained by the black and white mosaicked building. Like in the rest of the building — there are no straight lines; walls wave and floors roll. The floors are laid out with myriad flowing patterns in black and white that seem to go where they please — with no set direction. The tables are of all sizes and shapes — but in black lacquer as are the Thonet-style chairs used with them. The seat covers, however, are of assorted fabrics and patterns but all in black and white — like the amorphous walls that are also covered with the no-color mosaics.

Design: Hundertwasser
Photographer: MMP/RVC

In the center of the enclosed area is a circular service bar constructed of stones in a random and uneven pattern. It is topped with a black slate counter. Skylights let in the light and where the ceiling is lowered one can see that the construction is of timber beams. Hanging plants, bushes and trees are landscaped throughout to heighten the effect of nature in this black and white world which stimulates as it soothes and which also expresses the Hundertwasser credo and design philosophy.

ANTHROPOLOGIE

Wayne, PA

The coffee shop/cafe in the Anthropologie store is as unusual and different as the store itself. Anthropologie is a life-style concept store with a distinctive mix of apparel, home furnishings, garden products and gifts for "the sophisticated urban customer." The sensibility of Anthropologie is decidedly imaginative with a heightened appreciation of the world both natural and man-made.

This former car dealer's showroom of 9500 sq. ft. underwent minor interior demolition and structural elements like steel columns, girders and trusses were revealed — and they became part of the new store's look. Expansive skylights were added, where necessary, to insure abundant natural light. Throughout one sees many of the building's original materials like the terra cotta facing, the stamped tin ceilings, walls of brick and layered plaster. From the range of neutral colors and worn finishes came a new complementary palette; flooring that shifts from graystone to old wood planking to terra cotta tiles; walls of rough pigmented plaster applied in visible layers; ceilings punctuated with galvanized metal piping scoured of its shiny finish before installation. All this results in "a high touch rather than high tech sensibility."

Fixtures were fabricated out of fallen trees and tree limbs and birch and pine trunks can be seen standing in oxidized steel bases while supporting barn wood shelves or hang rods fashioned out of natural branches. Up front, near the main street windows, is the cafe with its unmatched collection of chairs and tables and the weathered wood bar topped with zinc. The tables are casually set out around the unusual, oval-shaped pool covered with colorful ceramic and crockery tile mosaics. "It brings a subtle suggestion of movement and tranquility to the space" as the gurgling fountain plays a tune of its own.

Anthropologie is "a place where customers can come to shop but also have a cup of coffee and hang out with their neighbors."

Design: PMPEI, A.D., New York, NY
Photographer: Tom Crane Photography

Design: Interspace Time, Tokyo, Japan

KINTETSU BISTRO/CAFE
Kintetsu Dept. Store, Nara, Japan

Interspace Time, a Tokyo and Los Angeles based architectural and design firm was chosen for the unique challenge of creating an entire department store in Japan. Contrary to the usual practice — no other firm, domestic or foreign, worked on any part of this project.

The concept of a European resort hotel was developed for the look of the 380,000 sq. ft. store with retailing on seven levels including the market in the Basement which was shown in the previous chapter. "The intent was to provide the customers with a feeling of warmth and elegance while shopping Kintetsu." To initiate a "welcoming" gesture upon entering the store, this inviting bistro/cafe was designed on the first floor (the ground level) which is most unusual since, in Japan, most restaurants and food facilities are set either in the basement or in the penthouse floors.

Apparent in the Bistro/Cafe is the palette of natural woods and light colors along with "the traditional styled architectural detailing." The floor is laid with squares of creamy marble and the elegantly-styled chairs are upholstered in a honey beige fabric.

The fine woods appear on the table tops and on the framework of the aforementioned chairs. Traventine covers the feature wall behind the cash desk which is a rich terra cotta color topped and based with the vanilla colored marble. "The end result is an elegant and detailed image creating a strong aesthetic identity translated into a time honored classic."

Blue Note Bar

Beck's Dept. Store, Cologne, Germany

For a complete change of tempo and mood we swing over to the Blue Note Bar which is located in the Beck's Dept. Store in Cologne and was named after a famous New York jazz club. This cafe was designed by Mathias Thoerner Design as part of the design of the 65,000 sq. ft. store. It is situated on a raised platform and is conveniently located adjacent to the music department.

The challenge to the designers was to get as much bar seating as possible into this 200 sq. ft. space which is separated from the sales floor of the store by the three inverted cone-shaped columns and the curved ramp. The bar counter is made of zinc, stainless steel and black stained wood. The sharp "V" of the counter not only maximizes the bar seating — it also creates an interesting visual effect. A glass brick wall separates the bar the work space next to it.

The bar service includes coffee, pastries and snacks and its being a neighbor of the music department ensures background music which in a way invites shoppers to partake of the "easy social atmosphere" in the retail setting.

Design: Mathias Thoerner Design, New York, NY

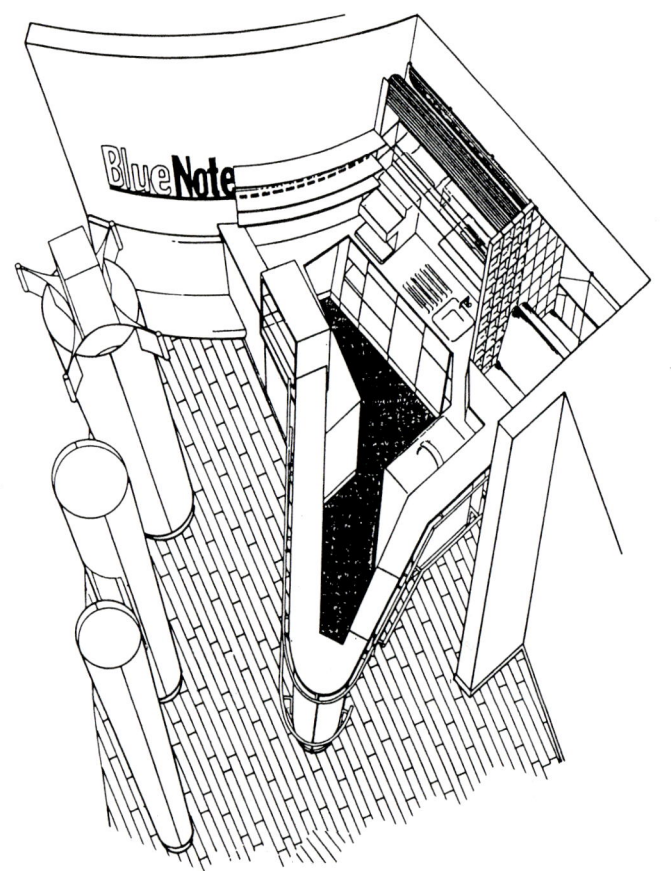

Design: Clodagh
Photographer: Daniel Aubry

FELISSIMO TEA ROOM
Felissimo, W. 56th St., New York, NY

The tea room at Felissimo — a most unusual and talked about store located in the 1901 Warren & Witmore townhouse on W. 56th St. — is a 42-seat treasure located on the top floor of the building. It shares the space with an art gallery and the fact that fully a quarter of the total retail space of the Felissimo store is devoted to the tea room/gallery makes it uniquely "Japanese." According to the designer, Clodagh, in Japan the retailer feels he "must give something back to the public — a place for culture beyond commerce."

The original concept for this tea room was to be a "calm haven" with an ambience suggestive of Viennese coffee houses where a coffee drinker can sit for hours — to read — to relax — to enjoy the pleasant passage of time.

A series of artists were commissioned to create the soft, warm and subdued ambience in rich, earthy colors with "eroded and patinated" surfaces — all to be enjoyed under the golden light. Oval tables of natural wood and tall, straight-backed chairs and high-backed upholstered banquettes are added to create an inviting quality to the space. The dramatically curved tea bar of rusted steel has etched into it the names of the various teas. In keeping with the theme, an abstract tea leaf design is drawn on the gently "aged" walls. In addition, the designer has seen to it that the tea room is stocked with books and current magazines for the convenience of the tea drinkers.

KAPPELI
Cafe/Brew Pub, Helsinki, Finland

The Cellar Pub is on the lower level of the Kappeli restaurant in Helsinki. The architectural details and decorations are left over from the 19th century structure that was originally built here as a "pleasure house" where one could obtain cakes and soft drinks. The designer, Errki Jaatinen, incorporated the very old with the new for interest and contrast as he and the architects restored this beautiful old building. Shown here is the oldest part which is now the Pub, and it features the two meter high brass and copper fermenting tanks which were originally built in Vienna many, many years ago. Directly in front is a sophisticated, new curved bar with high stools. The bar is constructed of green marble and black maple wood and it conveniently hides the top system and sink.

According to the designers, "Most of the European 'crewpubs' I have seen have been quite traditional and since there are no restrictions on breweries in Finland, I tried to do something new. Since the dignified old interior of Kappeli is so different, I introduced some new style elements in the 'crewpub' to complement it."

The new lighting system helps to create a warm and inviting ambience and it also enhances the "romantic" artwork on the wall which tells the story of how beer is brewed in a series of vignette paintings.

Design: Erkki Jaatinen
Photographer: Lauri Aitolahti

CAFE NINA
Helsinki, Finland

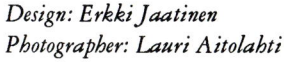
Design: Erkki Jaatinen
Photographer: Lauri Aitolahti

Located at point "zero" in the Main Railway Station in Helsinki is the Cafe Nina — a busy cafe for busy people. Because of its situation and because it is just above a heavily traveled underground station, all the materials used in the construction and decoration had to be durable.

The cafe is designed to seat 83 patrons and the self service cafe also features an open kitchen. The original cafe was dark and dreary and mostly patronized by "older" people. The designer had to affect a more up-beat and "younger" image in the remodeling of this space to attract a larger audience.

By making use of the two entrances into the cafe it was possible to plan two symmetrical self service lines in front of the open kitchen. The floor is paved with toast colored ceramic tiles and a raised platform was added which is finished with hardwood panels and steel balustrades. For furnishings, the designer selected small-scaled chairs to go with the wood and steel tables. The counters are lacquered nd finished with laminate panels and stainless steel bands.

This new Cafe Nina is now a "station area cafe that has been accepted by all kinds of people and it's become quite popular." In addition to coffee, tea and salads, there are assorted fresh and warm pastries prepared in the open kitchen.

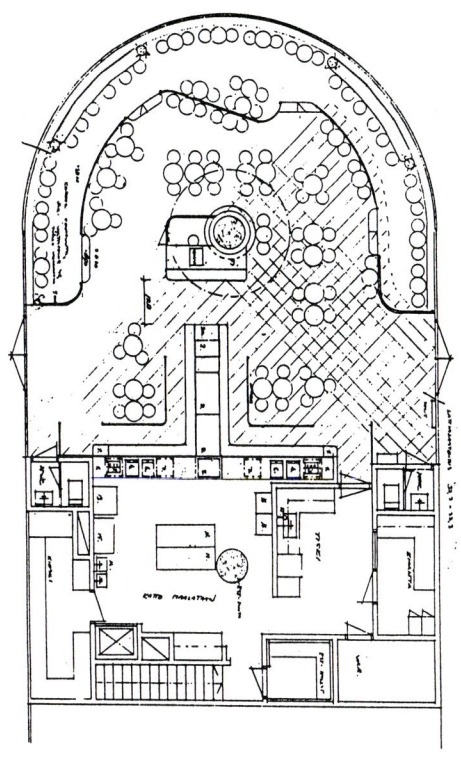

CAFFE TAZZA
Minneapolis, MN

The client is expanding its coffee house presence in the Twin City market (Minneapolis and St. Paul) in anticipation of increased competition in the new trend towards coffee houses and bars. The Caffe Tazza is the new answer and it was designed by Shea Architects of Minneapolis. This shop is located in Calhoun Square which is a popular uptown part of the city and also offers a diverse retail atmosphere. The area also attracts a sophisticated, fun-loving, ready-to-try-anything type of customer.

The cafe was designed with "eclectic detailing from several European influences" to take advantage of the diversity of the area and the people who shop Calhoun Square. Since the design is a prototype of future Caffe Tazza's, the designers had to establish standards and elements that could be incorporated into the future sites.

According to the design firm, "The space's architectural detail, finish selection, and ornamentation were manipulated to recreate a store several decades old." Ornate iron grills, gates and balustrades are used with the curlequed black wire chairs and gray marble-topped tables in a setting that combines "stone" arches and faded flocked wallpapered walls decorated with gilded frames and brass appliques. A small, raised wood-floored platform creates a secondary seating area and it is contained within a black wrought iron railing.

In addition to the flame shaped bulbs that hang down from the blacked-out ceiling, there are spots that wash the walls and highlight the food displayed in and on the counters and the shelves behind.

Design: Shea Architects, Minneapolis, MN

JONATHAN MORR ESPRESSO BAR
New York, NY

This smart and stylish Espresso Bar is located on Sixth Ave. and W. 57th St. in New York City — only a street away from Carnegie Hall and the New York City Center. It was designed by the well known restaurant designers, Jay Haverson and David Rockwell of New York City.

The designers have kept the interior clean and minimal with no extraneous ornamentation or decoration. The "stars" here are the coffee, tea, espresso, sandwiches, and pastries served all day from the curved, copper-covered bar in the rear of the long, narrow space. The bar is set askew — on an angle — from the long axis of the plan. Triangular-shaped waste bins are incorporated into the walls and they are outlined in stainless steel Throughout — in keeping with the angled placement of the bar — diagonals are used to outline and define the space like the green walls and ceilings that appear along the way to divide the space into a series of related areas.

On one wall, a pale terra cotta colored counter sawtooths its way across the beige wall and on the opposite wall there are a series of really small table rounds that are supported off the wall on curved metal pipes. These are for the convenience of the standing patrons. For those who would sit, there are some smartly-styled high black stools. The lighting fixtures repeat the circular motif of the individual wall tables in contrast to the sharp diagonal lines previously mentioned.

Design: David Rockwell & Jay Haverson
formerly of Haverson Rockwell, New York, NY

Papi Luis Cafe
East Village, New York, NY

The East Village in New York City has, for some decades, been considered the real "Bohemia" of New York; the real hip place to shop, to eat, and to see experimental theater. In contrast to the "hippy," "Grateful Dead" and "grunge" image that seems to ooze out of many of the local establishments, it is unique to find this white on white oasis call Papi Luis

The Coffee Bar was conceived by Glenn Hanna as a "late nineties coffee bar" — "bold and futuristic." According to Mr. Hanna, "People say the place looks very Milanese, but it's actually apple-pie American Modernism. Saarinen, Geary, Ames — the inspiration's all there — with a little Jetson and Barbarella thrown in. It's impressionistic with a lot of sensual active form."

A convoluted ceiling rolls along overhead in a space that is almost totally white on white except for some light natural colored wood accents that appear on the table tops. The folding chairs are chrome and clear plastic — adding no weight to the design. The flattering light is warm and it illuminates the wall panels and the artwork that creates a frieze over the white upholstered banquette. In addition there is a cylindrical lamp of stainless steel standing atop a long oval table that is equipped with tall bar stools.

"It's not Leather — Western — not Post-Modern — not frenetic. Just an ethereal place to meet, laugh, eat and exchange substantial ideas" over sandwiches, salads, desserts and, of course, coffee, cappuccino and espresso. "It's very late nineties."

CAFETERIAS & SELF-SERVICE FOOD AREAS

Deutsches Museum Cafeteria
Munich, Germany

Deutsches Museum Cafeteria

Munich, Germany

In the previous chapter on Coffee Bars/Shops and Cafes, we showed the Cafe at the Deutsches Museum which is one of the three food areas in this museum.

The restaurant shown here features a cafeteria-style service and the foods are presented on stainless steel and beech veneered counters that form a sweeping arc at one end of the space. Blue is the major accent color in this area and it completes the primary color scheme that was selected for the different dining spaces.

The floors are finished with blue/green granite and speckled terrazzo. The emphatic round columns are given even greater prominence in the design scheme by being increased in circumference and treated with the steely blue/green color. The quieter scheme was selected to be "meditative and soothing" — to "inspire repose and contemplation."

The designer played with curves to enhance the comfortable and relaxed ambience of the restaurant. It starts with the massive cylindrical columns and then there is the giant sweep forward in the food service area with a handsome beech wood and stainless steel, circular, soft drink unit in the center of the area — serving as a hub for the space. The silver and condiment service are incorporated into the bold curve of the matte and shimmering stainless steel counter that is built around one of the giant columns.

The windows wrap around much of the seating area so that the diner can enjoy the food along with the view. To supplement all of the natural light, there are recessed incandescent spots lined up on the ceiling. The food service area is also illuminated with the recessed incandescents plus some fluorescents.

Design: Mathias Thoerner Design, Inc., New York, NY

IL FORNAIO CUCINA EXPRESSA
Costa Mesa, CA

This project brings Il Fornaio's corporations's version of an Italian fast food operation to Orange County, CA by "combining the convenience and economy of cafeteria-style service with the elegance and drama of a European dining atmosphere."

To envision this, the company turned the project over to the architectural design firm, Backen Arrigoni & Ross, that, in turn, created this 4400 sq. ft. combination cafeteria/marketplace with a full take-out menu service. Inspired by an old Italian market hall, they defined the space "by the rhythm of broad arched openings" which complemented the grandeur inherent in the 29 ft. high ceilings of the space.

The kitchen exhibition cook line and service line co-exist with the public dining (70 persons inside) beneath the large, light filled, coffered ceilings. For a more intimate dining experience — in a secluded atmosphere — one can dine in the west dining hall.

The materials that were selected for the project "reinforce the owner's desire to maintain a refinement and elegance typically not associated with the efficiency of cafeteria-style service." The floor is laid with terra cotta tiles and there is a deep base cuff of travertine stone. The natural gray veneer plaster walls are accented with a rich Tuscan red mahogany trim and birdseye maple is used for highlighting. The counter tops and table tops are made of limestone. Custom made light fixtures are used throughout the space and authentic Italian artwork is lavishly applied to the walls of the restaurant.

Design: Backen Arrigoni and Ross, Inc.,
San Francisco, CA
Principal in Charge: Howard Backen
Project Manager: Ken Catton
Project Designer: Chris Von Eckartsberg
Project Architect: Chris Tons
Photographer: Douglas Dun

An entrance piazza with ivy covered windscreen and trellis provides a dramatic entrance way to Il Fornaio. It also serves for an out-of-doors eating area for about 50 patrons in the garden-like setting where the diners are sheltered from the wind and the sun.

This award-winning project does exactly what Howard Backen, principal in charge, wanted the design to accomplish; "I wanted a concert goer in black tie to feel as comfortable pushing through a tray as would an office worker at lunch time." This was accomplished by "the clean, classical look — an abstraction of traditional Italian interiors" and the use of fine materials and refined detailing.

Among the many awards heaped upon this project is the Golden Key Award for 1993 by *Hospitality Design* magazine.

CAFE BRIACCO

High St., Boston, MA

Design: Bergmeyer Design Associates, Boston, MA
Project Architect: Michael R. Davis/Doug Coots/Christine Canning
Photographer: Lucy Chen

The owners and managers of the Travelers Realty Investment Co. and Spaulding and Slye recognized the need for "a bright, active cafe to serve breakfast and lunch to their office tenants and to enliven the building's lobby."

Since the restaurateur, Brian Lesser, proposed a varied and updated Italian menu of salads, pastas, foccacia bread, pizza, and baked calzones, it was felt that the design should reflect the menu and be warm, Mediterranean in style — but decidedly contemporary in execution. The design team drew their inspiration from the "innate Italianess" of the Botticino marble that is used in the decoration of the building. Thus the designer's color and materials palette reflected the color and look of the marble. In this way the designers were able to keep the feeling of the cafe compatible with the imposing, cathedral-like lobby.

The design was executed as a series of contrasting themes; natural clean finish casework was overlaid with red aniline dye in an overscaled geometric pattern of triangles and diagonals. Artistic paint finishes describe large volumetric solids relating to the office building's structure while thin ceiling planes are simply painted and pierced with custom light fixtures. Bright and focused lighting contrasts with dark voids in the ceiling that open up to the building's mechanical systems.

Also based on the flooring of the lobby — but with a change — are the rotated grids of porcelain ceramic tiles which are separated by bands of marble mosaic; the same stone is used on the floor. To successfully complete the job in this 2100 sq. ft. space, the architects/designers combined drywall with painted finishes with maple veneered casework and counters decorated with red triangles and stainless trim. The specially-designed tables are topped with laminates.

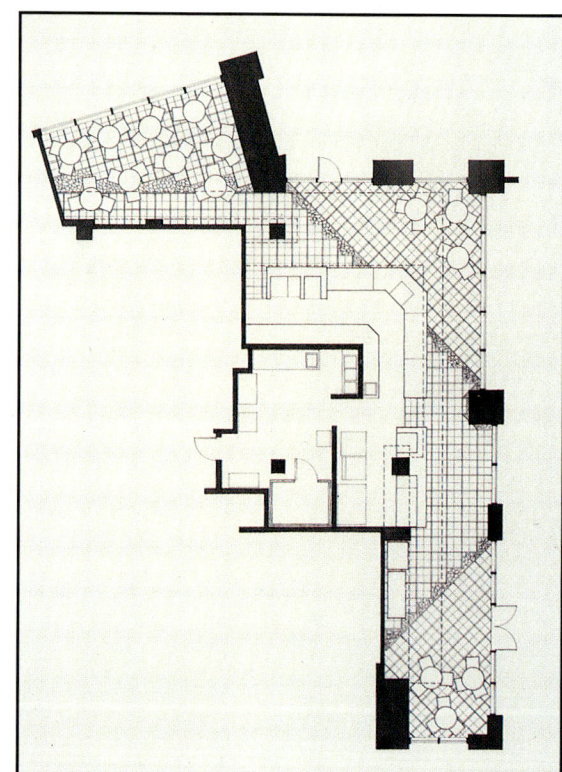

The Salad Bowl
Times Square, New York, NY

This take-out and self-service cafe/cafeteria which features freshly prepared salads, frozen yogurt and light fare is situated in the heart of Times Square. It is surrounded by a multitude of nationally known fast food chains. For this "unknown" operation to compete and succeed, it had to express a "combination of fun and excitement along with an appealing display of food items" to appeal to the largely tourist traffic.

The display counters and open kitchen are all configured in the front of the space to present the maximum amount of product exposure and activity towards the narrow store front. A perforated, back-lit, "serpentine shroud" above the open kitchen creates a major point of interest in the store's front area. Somewhat inspired by a recent re-reading of Alice in Wonderland, Hugh Boyd, the architect/designer, created a fantasy courtyard where the seating is arranged around giant pieces of fruit and oversized crockery shapes detailed with Matisse-like, still-life images.

By using large, carefully decorated shapes, the designer could economize on the remaining fixtures and furnishings — and thus stay within the limited budget. The floor is a sand and epoxy paint finish and the low walls are treated with a textured acrylic coating. Plywood chairs, originally designed by Alvar Aalto, are used with the birch plywood-topped tables which are finished with an industrial clear coating. "The simplicity of the furnishing and finishes is very much in keeping with the style and presentation of the food."

A higher proportion of the budget was spent on lighting the store's seating area since it is located far in the rear of the deep, narrow, and windowless space. It needed to be bright and spacious in feeling if it were to draw the patrons in.

Design: Boyd Associates, Montclair, NJ
Hugh Boyd

The Denver Salad Bar
Denver, CO

Though the architect/interior design team has collaborated on four other Denver Salad Bars in the past, this new one "maintains the clean crisp image" of the others though the designers have fine-tuned the basic concept and made minor modifications.

The self-service, cafeteria-style, 5000 sq. ft. restaurant has as its main focal attraction, the 75-item salad bar. In addition, the diner can have sandwiches, soups, muffins, and baked potatoes.

The setting is light and summery with a palate of rich pastels such as lavender, aqua, coral, peach, and lots of white and soft gray. According to the interior designer, Lisa Gallun, "the pastel colors lighten up the space and give it a vibrant, contemporary look," which is further enhanced by the neon signage that sparkles through the generally warm ambient incandescent lighting.

The traffic pattern of the self-service line up is determined by the angular design of the long salad bar and the food stations around the bar. Adding to the color and the summery festive quality of the project are the canvas hangings that are suspended from the ceiling grid which also carries the track lighting. Beyond — the ceiling has been painted black. The banners highlight the salad bar and they are also used in the outdoor dining patio along with awnings and fabric panels lashed onto the railings.

Design: Architect: *Harvey M. Hines, AIA, Boulder, CO*
Interior Design: *Gallun Design: Denver, CO*
Photographer: *Andrew Kramer, AIA*

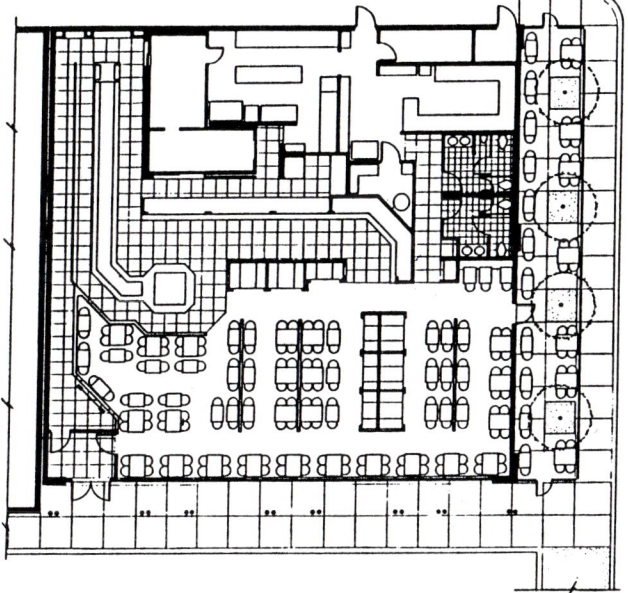

Ceramic tiles in lavender and pale gray cover the low dividing walls between the pastel laminated tables and the upholstered chairs that also tie in with the overall color palette. To add a sense of intimacy in the seating area, there are wide, flat cone-shaped pendant lamps suspended over some of the tables and matching wall fixtures send light up and down the wall. Paintings and graphics by local artists are used to decorate the sitting area. Throughout, the floor is laid with pale gray ceramic tiles which are randomly accented with pink tiles like the ones that face the service counters.

99

SOUPER SALADS
Tempe Center, Tempe, AZ

Souper Salads is a chain of fast food restaurants — self-service — located throughout the Southwest and Texas. "Clean & Simple" are the key words in the language of design in a Souper Salads operation.

This shop, in the Tempe Center, was designed by Sixty First Pl. Architects and it features a soup/sandwich counter, an extensive help-yourself salad bar, and comfortable seating for the patrons. The color scheme is coral, terra cotta, and pale pearl gray, accented with white. Terra cotta tiles pave the traffic aisle and self-serve area, while the seating area is carpeted in a dark, patterned broadloom. The seats are set in groups of tables and booths to one side of the coral/terra cotta colored dividing partition and the drop lights over the tables are fitted with incandescent lamps while the fixtures at and above the food service areas are halogen — "to bring out the natural colors and textures" of the foods.

Giant murals in rich earthy colors decorate the long wall behind the salad bar. Teal and white signs are used at the serving counter in the rear to designate what foods are available at which station.

Design: Sixty First Pl., Architects, Scottsdale, AZ

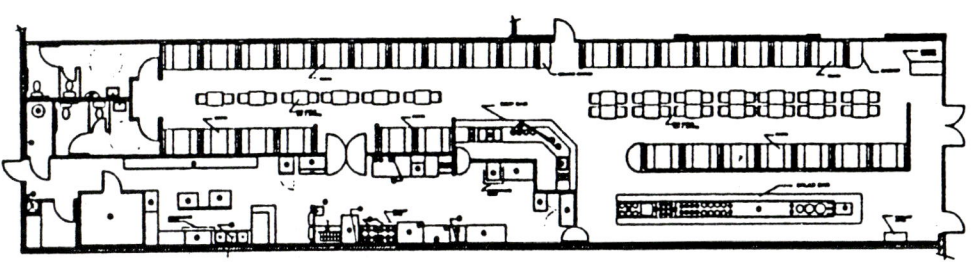

Food Garden Cafe
Selfridge's Dept. Store, Oxford St., London, England

The 350-seat cafeteria/restaurant is the "crowning achievement" of the refurbishment of the eastern end of this noted Oxford St. department store in London. The newly-installed escalators bring the shoppers up to the center of the fourth floor and the dramatic vista of this area.

The concept behind the Food Garden Cafe centers on "an abundant display of fresh produce and the cooking and serving of fresh food to order in front of the customer who is thus involved directly in the theater and fun of the food production." The design that resulted after extensive research in Switzerland takes advantage of minimizing the need for providing cooking facilities behind the scenes. Though there is a wide range of food offered, the elements of service and personal contact with all of the staff — including the chefs — is "enormously enhanced over a traditional, self-service, restaurant or food court."

Quality finishes and sparkling colors are used throughout with the terra cotta and stone floors used to link the whole space together. The solid beech "servery counters" with granite work surfaces house the sophisticated, but unobtrusive, cooking equipment.

Verandah-type wood screens with fret cut-out motifs, tropical style plantings, a Dufy-esque mural, William Tillyer paintings and decorative ceramic elements all combine to create "a spacious and relaxed" cafe setting.

Natural daylight pours in through the windows that are part of the cafe's setting as are the unobstructed views from this fourth level vantage point. When the sun fails to appear, the recessed incandescents in the ceiling are more than adequate to the task of providing the desired ambient light.

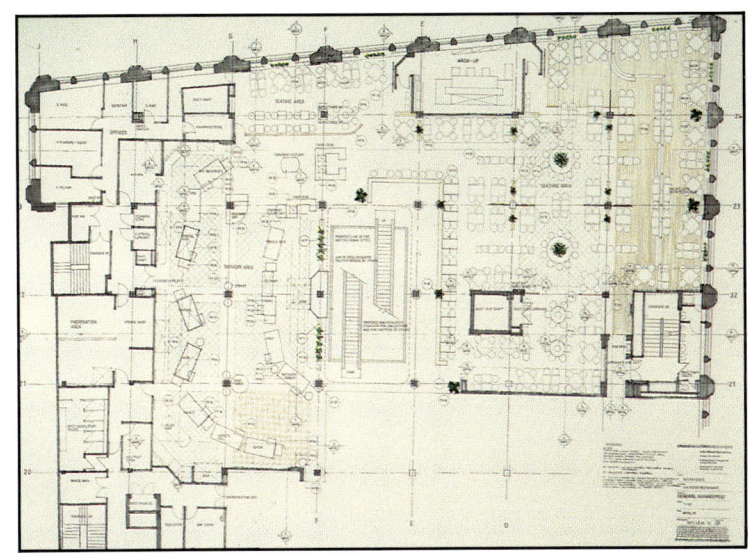

Design: John Herbert Partnership, London, England

Winter Garten

KaDeWe Dept. Store, Berlin, Germany

Situated under the glorious new addition to the famous KaDeWe Department Store is this sprawling Winter Garten, cafeteria-style restaurant. The new addition is the fabulous glass skylight — a glass and steel barrel vault that is 70 meters long and 11 meters high, and it turns the seventh floor of the store into a vast winter garden or conservatory filled with myriad hanging plants, flowering shrubs and trees in giant planters. Placed in and around the green landscaping are the many tables provided for the shoppers who can enjoy the view of Berlin along with the vast variety of foods.

This believable "stage set" was designed by the German architect designer, Rolf Zahetbauer who is also an Oscar-winning movie film set designer. The floor is laid with large white ceramic tiles banded in a pronounced angled grid by black tiles. The service counters and self-service stands out in the center of the food area are decorated with a chevron motif of aqua on white laminate — accented and trimmed with light, natural wood. In keeping with the barrel vault overhead, the arch motif appears in the decor of the spade; atop the individual service counters stainless steel frame is filled with a plastic panel that carries the name of the type of food available below is applied in white. Fresh flowers and exquisite arrangements of food decorate the buffet/salad bar/dessert bar.

At the opposite end of the floor, under a giant sun design of ceramic tiles and TV monitors is a long, snaking bar for those who require more than coffee, tea, or mineral water.

Design: Rolf Zehetbauer
Photographer: MMP/RVC

SANDWICH BOX
Safeway plc., Aylesbury, England

Safeway plc. is a large supermarket chain in the United Kingdom and they asked the London-based design firm of Virgile & Stone to collaborate with them and their food consultant, Prue Leith, to devise a new concept for the in-store, catering facilities. The end result of that collaboration is the Sandwich Box which is shown here. It is a self-service customer cafe which offers a selection of interesting combination sandwiches and sausages — "presented in attractive paper packaging and prepared and assembled to order."

"The design projects a modern and simple approach creating a light and fresh atmosphere to reflect the character of the products on offer with none of the cheapness usually associated with fast foods." The designers put heavy emphasis on the stainless steel finished counter presentation area which also incorporates a grill area. The flooring is a combination of wood in the seating area and ceramic tiles up around the service counter. In addition to the diner-style, upholstered, high-backed benches with rectangular tables, and between them there are the light-looking round tables with laminate tops and terrace-style, pull-up chairs.

Design: Virgile & Stone, London, England

Simple, but effective, counter displays plus an extensive graphics and signage program color the space and the paper packaging which was designed as part of the graphics program helps to "create a colorful and sophisticated approach to fast food corporate identity." A second site for another Sandwich Box is already in work with further sites being planned for the very near future.

The Good Earth
Galeria, Edina, MN

This ecological, environmental and health oriented cafeteria style restaurant is one of the several Good Earth operations located in Minnesota. This one is located in the very up-scaled Galeria in Edina — a suburb of Minneapolis — where it is surrounded by fine fashion and home furnishing shops. The concept behind the operation and the food offered appeals to the sophisticated audience who visits this one level, sprawling shopping center that has no food court.

Just off the main aisle of the mall, the shopper is assaulted by the smell and sight of the freshly-baked breads, rolls, pastries, and cakes displayed in slick, self-illuminated cases which are trimmed with light, natural oak and deep, forest green — the logo color of The Good Earth. The same color scheme is continued in the seating area beyond the tiled entrance/service area. Here, on a textured rich green carpet are upholstered banquettes and chairs covered with woven green fabric and the room is finished in a light, peach/beige color and more of the natural oak wood. Metal drop lights add their incandescent glow to the foods displayed up front and they also enhance the ambience of the seating area.

The feeling throughout is contemporary tempered with country casual warmth and charm. The dark green accents add to the sense of value as well as what the shop's name is all about.

Herald Cafe
Washington, DC

The 4000 sq. ft. self-service facility in the Herald Square building in downtown Washington, DC seats 75 persons and is open for breakfast and lunch, and also serves snacks throughout the business day. The designers created two distinct areas; one with bright lighting that surrounds the two long salad bars, and the hot food serving line and the other — with a lower lighting level — which affects a warmer and more serene ambience where the seating is located.

The food options are presented on an angle so that the full array of food is immediately visible to the patron coming down the stairs into this below street level restaurant. They can also see the seating available beyond. The designers created the Herald Cafe in a contemporary style and used simple materials and design elements to create "an exciting and entertaining dining environment." Several colors of ceramic tile decorate one of the walls and they "erode" away to abstract murals that affect the illusion of looking through the walls." The illusion is continued in the checkerboard patterned floor with a third color dropped in at random to break up the regularity of the motif. The floating ceiling repeats the checkerboard design with random voids doing what the third color tile did on the floor. Brightly painted red mechanical systems can be seen through the open spaces of the dropped ceiling with the black openwork grid.

Design: Brennan, Beer, Gorman, Monk/Interiors, New York, NY

Indiana State University Food Court

The Commons, Terra Haute, IN

We have come a long, long way from the dull and dreary school cafeterias of yesterday with the gray and flavor-drained, steamed-out foods served unappetizingly in uninviting and unfriendly settings. Today's students have options!

An excellent example of the new trends in school dining facilities is shown here and on the following pages. With the opening of The Commons in the Indiana State Univ. in Terre Haute, the university realized its goal of "offering our students, particularly the 3700 who have meal plan contracts, the finest college food service available anywhere in the country" (Paul Edgerton, V.P. for Student Affairs). The facility combines restaurant dining with fast food outlets for a generation of students brought up and nurtured in the food courts of malls.

In addition to the 120-seat, full-service restaurant, Generations, there are the "stands" where students can opt for the specialties provided by Burger King, Pizza Hut, and Taco Bell. Other food service operations in this food court setting include Subway Sandwiches, Mark Pi' Chinese Carry-Out, and Blondie's Cookies. "The brand name fast food outlets together with restaurant and the services available in the convenience store provide an attractive on-campus dining alternative to all members of the campus community."

Burger King, Pizza Hut, and Blondie's Cookies are each 750 sq. ft. spaces. Taco Bell is in a 600 sq. ft. space, while Mark Pi's Express fills the 550 sq. ft. allotted to it. The convenience store, the 1000 sq. ft. Campus Cupboard, features over 200 items ranging from toiletries and snacks to a dry cleaning service. This facility operates from 7 AM to 11 PM, seven days a week. All of these easily-recognized operations are set out like in a food court around the 926-seat mauve and blue dining area which is the core of The Commons.

According to Glenn Kvidahl, Food Service Director, "Part of the objective was to have a place for kids to gather and the Commons has become THE place to go," especially since the Commons is the only dining facility open on the weekends and it becomes "an excellent place to meet other students from all parts of campus on these days."

The "Foodstyles" plan developed by MMS includes Campus Credits and Commons Cash. The Campus Credits are used for admission to the Resident Dining Halls and the Common Cash (or Points) are used to purchase food in the Common's Food Court and the Convenience Store. A portion of all residence hall meal plans are in the form of Commons Cash so that the students can make use of the Commons retail food outlets.

Design: Marriott Management Systems Design & Development Group
Project Architect/Manager: Kent Rattan
Dir. Store Planning & V.M.: Ruth Crowley Jacinto

CALIFORNIA STATE UNIVERSITY CAFETERIA

Northridge, CA

The Hatch Design Group was commissioned to design the food service areas in the new, two-story addition on the west side of the existing university bookstore. It included creating a mini-food court which features El Pollo Loco, 31 Flavors, Southside Pizza, and Burger King, along with seating in the covered indoor/outdoor dining area which is located in the 32 ft. wide, sky-lit concourse.

"The focus of the design is the diagonal portion of the concourse which is oriented towards the main campus thoroughfare and attract students into the internal activity space and on through the concourse" to the seating area of the cafeteria. The color scheme is mainly gray and white for the floor tiles, table tops, and the service counters sparkled with bright and striking accents of red and yellow/gold. The padded seats are upholstered in red, and red laminates are used to face the service counters.

Design Firm: Hatch Design Group, Costa Mesa, CA
Principal in Charge: Richard Hatch
Project Manager: Rick MacCormack
Architect: Coleman/Cashey Arch. Inc.
Photographer: Larry Falke

American University Food Court

Washington, DC

Design: The Marriott Management Systems Design & Development Group
Project Arch./Mngr: Kent Rattan
Dir. of Store Planning and V.M.: Ruth Crowley Jacinto

A survey of the student body of A U in Washington, DC showed that what was wanted was more vegetarian foods and more self-service options, so the Marriott Management Systems, who are the caterers for the University, introduced a completely new concept in food offerings and design for the school cafeteria.

Marriott introduced over 20 self-service options which include "Wok Your Own" — a self-serve bar where students can stir-fry their own choice of shrimp, pork, chicken, several vegetables, two kinds of rice, and a choice of oils and spices; "Salubre Pizza" is a Marriott developed brand concept which offers freshly-made, personal pan pizzas with whole wheat crust; for those who like more spice in their life and diet MMS developed "Carlos Peppers" which offers Tex-Mex items including a self-service Mexican salad and hot entree bar along with make-your-own nachos, tacos, and burritos.

Each food stand was designed to suggest the kind of food being offered and since almost all are self-serve, the display, graphics, and signage were vital to the success of the new program in this unusual college cafeteria.

SONY MUSIC CENTER CAFETERIA

Santa Monica, CA

The Sony Music Complex in Santa Monica is headquarters for over 200 employees and the three buildings that surround an inner court in true Southern California "life-style" were designed along with the food facilities by Steven Ehrlich. The design of the unique complex which covers 100,000 sq. ft. was influenced by the "music notations and streamlined moderne architecture that flourished in Santa Monica during the 1930s" (*Interior Design Magazine*).

In addition to al fresco dining areas located in the landscaped inner court there is an enclosed cafeteria which is pictured here. The space is almost Spartan in its simplicity and in the open, neutrality of the design which is clean and contemporary. The designer left the corrugated ceiling, the industrial trusses and mechanical systems exposed and painted white like the dry wall construction of the space. A pre-finished oak with a weathered gray character was selected for the flooring while the open kitchen and the rear of the service area was paved with white ceramic tiles to complement the white laminates used on the counter fronts and table tops. The tables and the avocado-colored chairs were selected by Pizzulli Assoc. who were also responsible for the lobby and workstation furnishings.

The unusual decorative panels on the pristine walls were created as part of an art program at the Santa Monica School of Art and Design. The colorful collages of paper plates and napkins add color and verve to the otherwise cool space which is warmed up by the theatrical style lighting fixtures on the ceiling.

Design: Steven Ehrlich, Architect, Santa Monica, CA
Photographer: Tom Bonner

Dolce & Freddo
San Felipe at Voss, Houston, TX

This is the second location for the popular Dolce & Freddo shops in Houston and it is located in a triangularly-shaped building that was originally a savings and loan bank. The long side of the triangle is fully glazed and the original cladding material on the building's exterior is wood siding.

In the course of remodeling the space, the second story of the building was opened up and a balcony was affected which now sits partially over the main dining area on street level. The existing entry was relocated and there are now two portal-style entrance-ways made of black granite. A large wood deck was added onto the wood faced structure "so that customers can hear the cars race by and smell the fumes — just like in Italy" — says the client.

The new interior space has floors covered with granite, Italian ceramic tiles and Toli vinyl tiles while the long, impressive service counters are made of oak which has been stained red with aniline dye. The furniture is light and airy — reminiscent of patio furniture, so that the "outdoor" ambience is continued inside this Dolce & Freddo.

"The lighting was kept soft and unobtrusive" with PAR 36's used in the gypsum board ceilings. Pendant RLM fixtures with 2-19 lamps are hung over the black granite tables which recall the impressive pontils that are the entries into this cafe.

Design: Brand + Allen, Houston, TX
Design Team: Joel Brand and Michelle Bowers

General Accident Insurance Co. Cafeteria

Melville, NY

Design: Spectorgroup, North Hills, NY
Photographer: Mark Ross

Like the Sony Music Center, The General Accident Insurance Co. in Melville, NY required an up-scaled, bright and sparkling cafeteria that would refresh their employees both with food — and with a sense of renewed spirit.

The designers, Spectorgroup, derived their interior design concept for the cafeteria from the building's "strong structural elements and unique interacting forms." Rather than "hiding or working around architectural elements such as structural columns and oblique angles, the design team took advantage of these components to create an interesting and stimulating area.

Since the designers were constrained by a strict budget, they relied on a dramatic black and white color scheme dynamically underlined and scored with bright red accents. The bold black and white checkerboard vinyl floor and the decorative black lacquered, floor-to-ceiling grids allowed "a functional definition of space" while the ambient and task lighting further defined the circulation in the cafeteria and the dining spaces set apart.

Design: NBBJ, Seattle, WA
Photographers: David Hewitt & Anne Garrison

CHILDREN'S WAY CAFE
San Diego, CA

The cafeteria at the Children's Hospital and Health Center in San Diego is called "Children's Way Cafe" and the 3500 sq. ft. space was designed by NBBJ of Seattle. It not only has a seating capacity of 72, but there is an outdoor eating area attached to it which can accommodate more diners.

To make the cafe/cafeteria as appealing as possible to the children and yet comfortable and relaxing for the parents, the designers balanced "playful materials" and casework with a crayon box accent palette which is balanced by lots of soothing blue shades. The major casework includes an arched, segmented trash/recycling bin and a boat-like, multi-colored cash register island. The random recessed can light fixtures and the neon add to the bright, striking colors on the checkerboard patterned floors and the gaily finished columns. A serpentine red mesh "ruffle" follows the swelling curve of the wall that separates the dining area from the service area. The bright blue and aqua colors are repeated on the chairs in the seating area of the cafeteria where the off-white walls and table tops offer some reprieve for the adults from the onslaught of color up front and the red-faced counters in the food service area.

INFORMAL & THEMATIC DINING

AIRSTREAMS ROADSIDE CAFE
Avon, CT

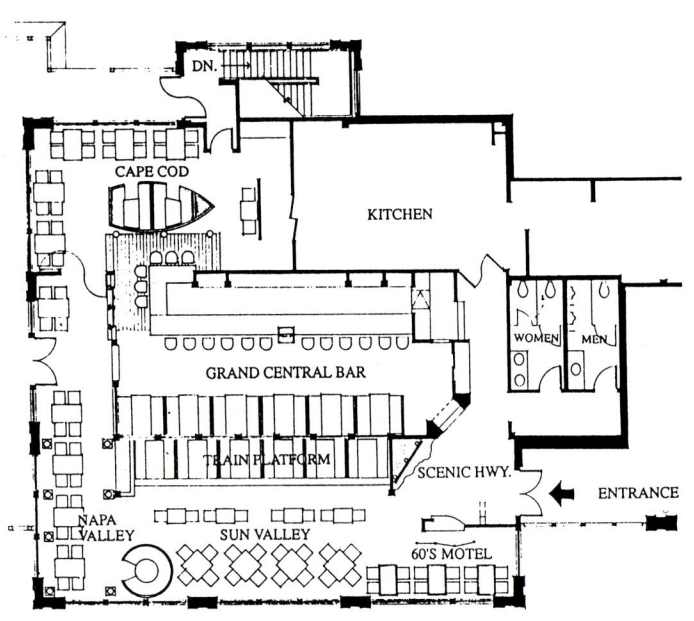

Design: Judd Brown Designs, Inc., Warwick, RI
Project Team: Michael Gilespie/Steven McMahon/Mark Palazio/
Lisa Simeone
Photographer: Warren Jagger

AIRSTREAMS ROADSIDE CAFE
Avon, CT

You can see the whole United States and never leave the charm and comfort of Avon, CT. The diner is invited to take an informal and fun-filled tour by just stepping off the dual highway that is simulated on the floor up front and enter into the imaginative wonders of Airstreams Roadside Cafe. At the entrance there is a giant roadside billboard illuminating a scene of a superhighway while the scraggly grass around its base is ornamented with odd hub caps. In addition there is a piece "architecture" that suggests the garish, neon infested roadside motels circa 1950 and over the entrance a sign that indicates that the diner has arrived at the City Limits of "Airstreams."

The first dining area, appropriately enough, has the look, feel, and smell — as well as color — of the roadside diners that still exist off the main highways that criss-cross the country. There are high backed, camel colored, naugahyde covered booths, a white tiled floor and black and white checkered seats pulled up to the gray linoleum topped tables. Red, yellow, and blue accents are added to brighten up the fun space.

Next on the "gastronomic tour" is a visit to Sun Valley ski resorts where amidst snowflakes on the sky blue ceiling and the snow white vinyl floor beneath, the diner can enjoy the old-fashioned travel posters and snow and ski memorabilia that has been crammed into this space along with the tables and chairs. For a change of scenery and climate — the diner can indulge in the warmth and charm of the vineyards of the Nappa Valley where a grape draped pergola becomes the focal object of the space. The final leg of the trip is back to the East Coast and up to Cape Cod with the decorative emphasis on lobster pots, fish nets, sea-faring objects and artifacts, weathered woods and shingles, captain's chairs and even a pair of anglers dangling up-side down overhead in an upturned boat.

The Grand Central Bar recalls the elegance and style that was once associated with rail travel — when it was the gracious way to go.

The long, narrow space looks like the old-fashioned Pullman cars with the antimacassared red banquettes, the lowered ceiling and the "faded rug" and brass stanchions that separate the seating area from the long mahogany bar with a terrazzo cuff that matches the black and white checkered terrazzo floor. Through the "windows" the diner can enjoy the "sights" of the Sun Valley area which is adjacent to the Grand Central Bar.

It is all aboard — gas up and tank up — for a truly unique dining adventure on the go.

Yellow Rose Cafe

Amsterdam Ave., New York, NY

Way out west — on the west side of Central Park, on Amsterdam Ave. in New York City, there is a real, Texas-style informal place to eat and drink — Texas-style.

The space is long and narrow, typical of the store front spaces one finds on Amsterdam Ave., and into it the designers, Spitzer & Associates, have crammed the bits and pieces of memorabilia that one associates with the big state of Texas. Here, too, one can feel the texture and respond to the color of the source of inspiration while one's sense of smell is assaulted — most deliciously — by the smell of fried chicken steaks, fried okra, and baked biscuits, soon to be drowned in cream gravy. Overhead the ceiling has the bye-gone-days look that is associated with stamped metal ceilings and below, the floor has been stained red and then wiped down to "antique" it before finishing it with polyurethane — for that burnished look.

A small bar space, only 9 ft. wide, welcomes diners up front and the bar is faced with oak tambour, and a painted, stepped motif cut out of plywood is applied over it as a decorative border. The stools are covered with faux pony skin fabric. Some of the collection of kitch memorabilia is used to decorate this area.

CAFE MED AT COCOWALK
Coconut Grove, Miami, FL

This flagship restaurant, designed by "Jack" Baum of Tree House Design, is the prototype for a chain of informal restaurants that are planned to be rolled out in North America and Europe. The owner's program required a space that was "suggestive of a long-established and somewhat worn, country or coastal cafe that one might find anywhere along the Mediterranean coast." The space also had to be warm and inviting — casual and bright — and be suited to settings like at Cocowalk which is an open air mall.

The design program called for an open kitchen, a wood burning pizza oven, and a holding bar that would also act as a serving bar. With these requirements, Baum tried to affect the ambience of a remote country market where the food display and preparation would be the main focus and the seating area would be like that of an outdoor cafe alongside the market. The 5000 sq. ft. space is divided into two by the central "street" which is actually a continuation of the open air arcade of the exterior of the Cafe Med. At one end of the "street" one can see the open kitchen and the pizza oven where the hood over the kitchen is made of oxidized and polished zinc. The same finishes are used on the bar which is to the right of the kitchen. A lattice grill acts as a cage to lock up the back bar after closing but during the open hours it is hooked to the ceiling and creates an awning-like element over the back bar. On the opposite side of the "street" is the seating area with the table tops stained deep green and accented with decorative tiles.

Overhead the ceiling is a mixture of rough hewn timber construction and stucco with custom, cone-shaped, pendant lighting fixtures of galva-

nized zinc. The perimeter lights are recessed with rings of colored, Italian Murano glass. The floor has a border of pre-cast "keystone" concrete tiles, like those used on the exterior plaza, and a field of hand-made, terra cotta tiles accented with occasional decorative, glazed tiles. Around the perimeter of the space is "a custom painted wood store front with stained glass accents that opens up to extend the restaurant out into the exterior plaza" where there is another 500 sq. ft. of seating area.

In addition, there is a 1000 sq. ft. free-standing, self-service, take-out outlet that is similar in style to the cafe which also faces the exterior courtyard.

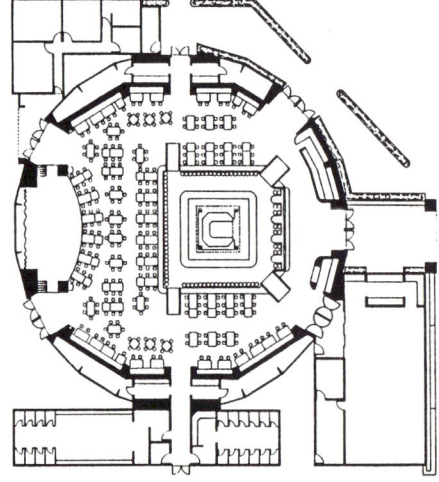

THE EARTH

Minato-Ku, Tokyo, Japan

The Suntory Company of Japan created a new beer called "The Earth." In order to introduce the new beer, the firm decided to tie it in with an "environmentally conscious" theme. The design challenge to Interspace Time was to create a temporary restaurant/cafe to market the beer. The design team came up with a 5/8 shere-like canvas and metal structure which suggests the roundness of the earth. The pre-fabricated structure was designed to stand for three months on an open lot in downtown Tokyo and then it would be dismantled and re-assembled in some other location.

The "theme" continues inside the yellow canvas sphere and here the design concentrates on the rapidly vanishing "Rain Forests" of South America. The informal diner can "experience a tropical forest environment that consumed a civilization of the past as an archaeologist would find in search of 'lost ruins.'"

Elements of South and Central America are meshed in the collage of bold, organic shapes, bright colors and rusted finishes. The "main stage" is a representation of a futuristic archaeological Indian ruins surrounded by over-scaled bull-horn torches." The structure over the bar is a "whimsical ancient beer distillery" that houses all the stage lights and the sound system. Spanish Mission architectural elements are also introduced into the soaring interior.

Up front, near the entrance, is an "action kitchen" where the diners-to-be can see authentic Brazilian food being prepared which they will later be able to enjoy as they listen to the live ethnic music.

Design: Interspace Time, Tokyo, Japan
Principal in Charge: Stome Usihidate
Design Team: Fred Hope/Robert Lowe/ Michael Labasan
Assoc. Interior Design: Tanseisha
Photographer: Jun Miromi

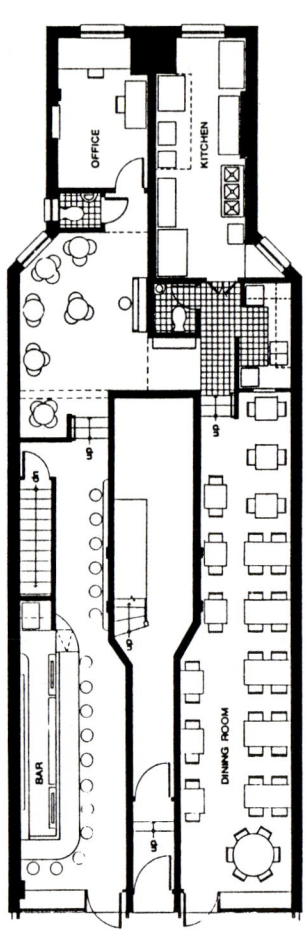

Design: Spitzer & Associates, New York, NY
Photographer: Georgina Bedosian

A few steps up and towards the rear of the space is the small dining area with the specially designed "animal skin" chairs and tables. Besides the cactus plants that appear in woven baskets and terra cotta pots, the main decorative elements are the old, but now working "Ranch Tavern" neon sign overhead and the 1940s, stand-up piano below it which is trimmed with assorted stickers, decals and cut-outs of the period.

The place is as friendly and welcoming and as Texas as the owner, Barbara Clifford, who brought her heritage with her up to Amsterdam Ave. Fred Clapper of Spitzer and Assoc. was able to give her the "setting" she desired.

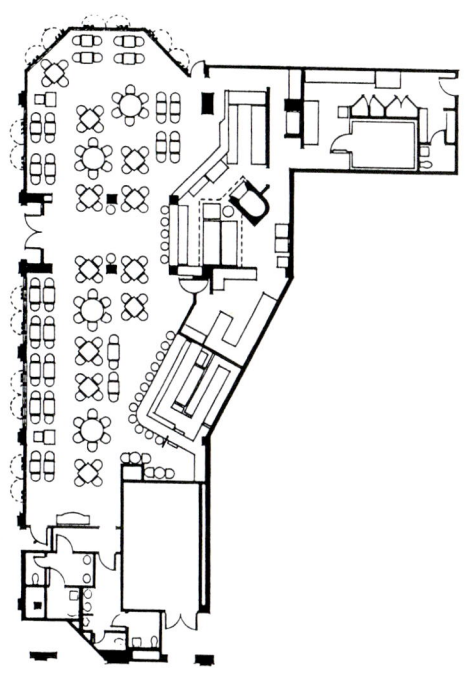

Design: Tree House Design, Ltd., New York, NY
Designer/Project Manager: Julius S. "Jack" Baum
Design Team: Karen Tappis/Greg Harry
Architect: M.C. Harry and Assoc., Miami, FL
Photographer: Karl Francetic, New Medford, CT

The Good Diner

W. 42nd St., New York, NY

The 3000 sq. ft. "diner" is located on W. 42nd St. and 11th Ave. in New York City. The clients stressed that they did not want the diner to be either "retro" or "trendy"; they just wanted a place where "simple, honest foods at a fair price" could be obtained in a neighborhood that was desperately in need of such an informal dining spot. Pentagram Design was retained to name, design, and provide a complete graphics program for the restaurant.

One partner "named" the restaurant — another drew the logo which is "a cup of coffee elevated to sainthood." This design was extended to menus, announcements, stationery and signage. A third partner, as the architect, conceived the interior as a "somewhat excessive collaboration of the ordinary 'vernacular' materials commonly used in diner construction." Therefore, the stools and banquettes are upholstered in bright, primary colored naugahydes and the floors and table tops are covered with three different types of linoleum. The "art program" consists of huge framed photocopies of "archetypical diner objects" like salt shakers, sugar dispensers and tea bags. As a decorative but useful device there is a series of 12 slightly different clocks used as a decorative frieze behind the counter.

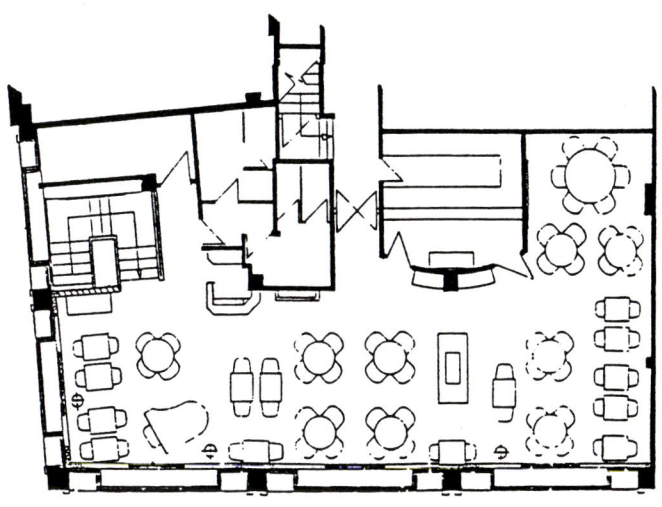

Design: Pentagram Design, New York, NY
Partner/Architect: James Hiber
Partner/Graphic Designer: Michael Bierut
Partner/Illustrator: Woody Pirtle
Designer: Lisa Cerveny
Arch. Asst.: Michael Zweck Bronner

Heartwise Express

Chicago Pl. Mall Food Court, Chicago, IL

"We wanted to create an atmosphere where people could enjoy health food while reflecting on the environment," says Keith Youngquist of the design firm of Aumiller Youngquist who created Heartwise Express as an informal health food restaurant alternative to the usual fast foods served in malls. The design team turned to unendangered and recycled woods, natural paints and stains, granite, glass, and ceramic tiles for the materials palette needed to create the four distinct dining settings in the restaurant. The areas are "pond," "cave," "forest," and "prairie."

"We positioned the column at the entrance to direct attention into the space" of 3600 sq. ft. which now features seating for 95. The column is richly encrusted with colorful glass mosaics and patterned with plant life and turtles. It also is designed to hold reading material and brochures relevant to the environment and nutrition. Just to the left of the column is a curving service bar made of antique heartwood pine which is topped with black granite. The walls behind the service counter is also panelled with wood and prominently displayed on the wall is the menu board.

The "pond" area is distinguished by the variegated blue and green ceramic tiles on the floor and the bright blue "sky-ceiling" above. The area is contained by a wood railing which frames a metal sculpture design of reeds. The walls of "cave" are rough and bumpy in texture and they are enhanced by the barely-perceptible animal drawings on the beige walls that are like the murals found in the prehistoric cave in the south of France. The painted glass panels over the banquettes in the "forest" are warm, golden, and mottled with the colors of autumnal foliage.

Throughout the seating is plywood chairs and the table tops are made of old, recycled woods such as pine, walnut, heartwood and American chestnut. "The display of these re-used wood products demonstrates the need to maintain our natural resources" and to add to the consciousness raising of the diners, each table top is stamped with the name of the species of wood that was used.

Design: Aumiller Youngquist P.C., Prospect, IL
Project Team: Keith Youngquist A.I.A., Greg Howes, Leigh Maravigli, Jeanne Mercer
Photographer: Steinkamp/Ballogg, Chicago, IL

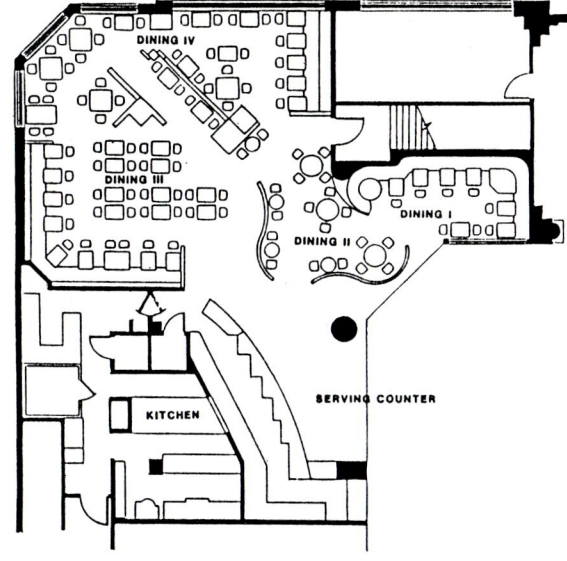

LOCAL-NO CHOL
Westgate Village, CA

The 1600 sq. ft. restaurant is located in the rural Westlake Village and the inspiration for Local-No Chol came from the difficulty one of the owners, Robert Bell, had getting the "right" food after his heart attack. This utilitarian yet contemporary up-scaled restaurant serves "heart-healthy food" — low in calories and no cholesterol.

The design team used economical plywood for the sleek geometric patterns on the walls and mixed in a black galvanized ceiling alive with bright spangles. Plywood and grain "awnings" are suspended out off the walls by means of turnbuckles and tension cables. Similar vertically-suspended panels carry the menu boards over the open kitchen and service bar. The table tops are made of natural plywood with galvanized metal inset strips which play off the angular designs on the walls and also add interest to the table tops. "The intentional sun-patterned wall sconces (designed by Don Sadler) are made of fiberglass and galvanized metal. These were incorporated into the design to fit the balance of the textured hand painted walls (Leslie Warren) of earthy yellow, burnt orange and cool ocean blue patterns for a sense of well being." To further get the "heart-healthy" message across, there are open grid, galvanized metal heart shaped sconces that have flickering orange flame lights.

According to Gina Muzingo, principal of Muzingo Associates, "The entire concept from menu to design to marketing is geared to energize the guests and have them leave with a sense of harmony knowing that they did something good for their bodies." The entire project was successfully completed on a very tight budget of $125 per sq. ft. complete.

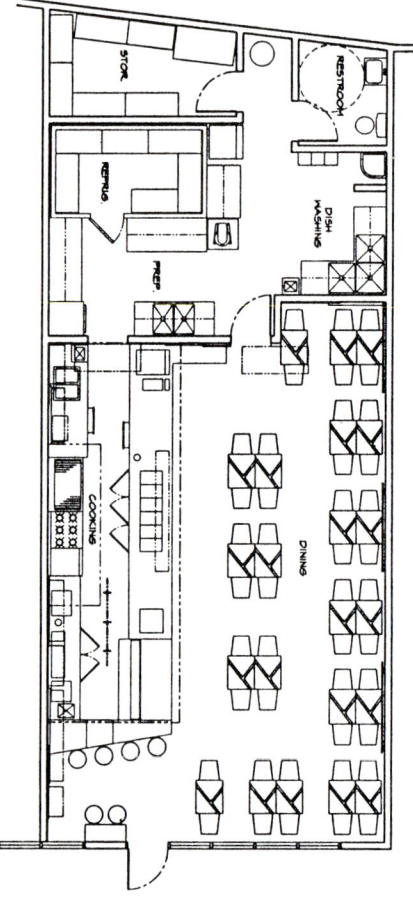

Design: Muzingo Associates, Los Angeles, CA
Project Team: Gina Muzingo & Jonathon Turnbull
Photographer: Alex Verticoff

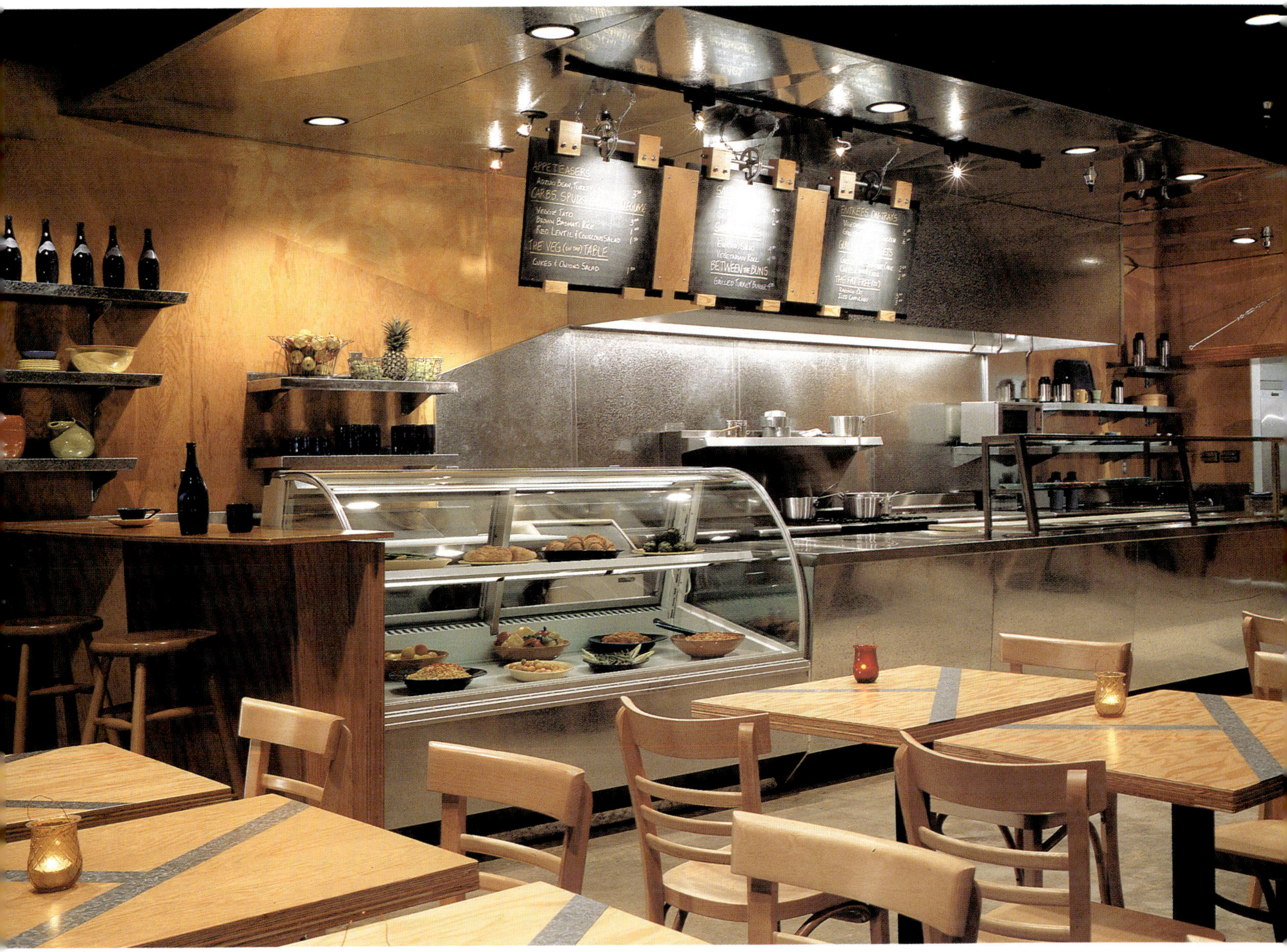

133

JOE ROCKHEADS
King St. W., Toronto, Ontario, Canada

The design firm, Hirschberg Design Group, started with the architectural "deck" stacked against them. They were faced with a 4800 sq. ft. below-street-level space that lacked street presence, a low ceiling, an L-shaped configuration, kitchen walls that created visual blocks that divided the area, three failed previous operations, and — a very restricted budget with which to turn things around.

The design solution began with the opening up of the ceiling to create interest and the conversation of the enclosed kitchen into an open one where the food preparation becomes part of the visual attraction of the restaurant. The dominant existing bar was scaled down and the designers re-used the existing lighting fixtures but dramatically improved the overall lighting of the space by introducing a new European low voltage, cable light system. The 230 lights "appeal to the human desire for light and air" and offset the negative effect of being below grade level. A directional floor pattern was introduced and by using "creative materials" they were able to achieve "an off-beat, light-hearted feeling of fun."

The rear area of the space, which had in previous operations been avoided is now in great demand since the redesign provides an idea meeting place for groups. A second curving stand-up counter also serves as an informal designator behind which groups can obtain a semi-private space consisting of service bar, pool table, seating and raised banquettes. It becomes a "separate but integral" part of the overall Joe Rockhead experience.

Design: Hirschberg Design Group, Inc., Toronto, Ontario, Canada

Some of the beverage suppliers provided approved artwork/advertising murals that eased up the client's budget for artifacts. There are two permanent murals (Absolut and Grand Marnier) and a semi-permanent chalk art mural that is redesigned bi-monthly. Still below street level and with limited street presence, this current reincarnation is alive and well — and thriving on King St. W.

Spinnakers

Queens Quay W., Toronto, Ontario, Canada

The waterfront location determined the ambience of Spinnakers which is located on the popular Queens Quay in Toronto. Though it is an extremely popular place to be in the summer, the owners wanted an interior that would encourage and sustain a year-round business. With a budget of $100,000, and a minimal three-week construction period, the Hirschberg design team came up with imaginative and inexpensive ways of maintaining a Mediterranean outdoor terrace theme indoors.

For the sake of budget and time, the designers relied on simple architecturally detailed partition walls which are at once functional and interesting and on the re-use of some of the existing fixtures and the terrazzo flooring. The new custom wall finishes were introduced that "resulted in an explosion of added color, texture, light, and energy." There is a feature wall with an etched fresco-like, Venetian plaster mural which carries through the water theme and also adds an historic European quality. This "encaustic" technique used on the mural utilizes wax and draws its inspiration from an ancient technique that employed beeswax in its execution. The result has "an aged and fossilized" feeling.

Design: Hirschberg Design Group, Toronto, Ontario, Canada
Faux Finishes: Atelier Danzig

The design team specified the "ironic juxtapositioning of material such as floor slate used as a bar top, canvas awnings facing inward and a galvanized steel bar front with natural wood enhancement. All this was to indicate "durability that if exposed to the elements would allow you to lift off the roof and invite the gentle breezes that blow in through the wall that was opened up by the installation of sliding glass doors — to evoke the desired customer response.

In keeping with the seaside theme, the railings are traditional fish net executed in metal to further promote "the casual, non-rigid, loose, flowing and sculptural form and feeling" that the designers envisioned as Spinnakers.

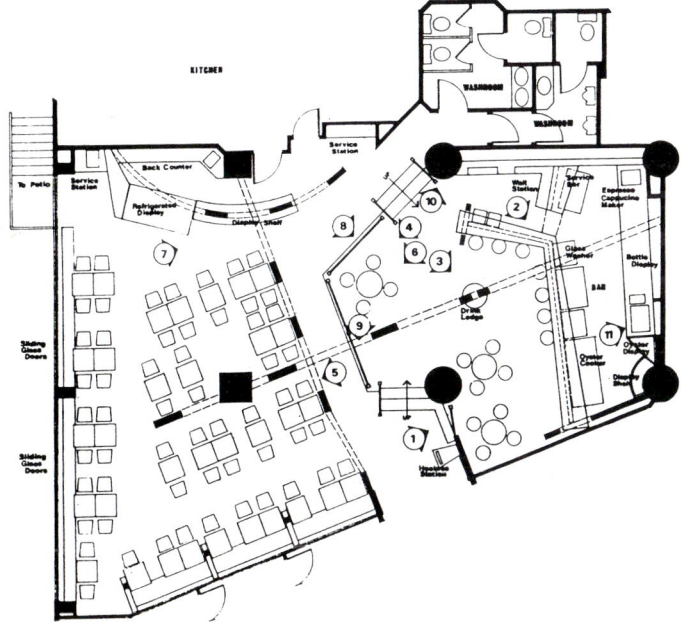

Design: Dorf Associates, New York, NY
Principal: Martin Dorf
Graphic Designer: Preston Williamson Design
Photographer: Maseo Ueda

CHECKERS
Philadelphia, PA

Like Joe Rockhead's, this 3000 sq. ft. restaurant renovation was undertaken to "create a new and strong identity" that was to turn the previously dark and non-obtrusive location into a "destination" and — to do this transformation on a low budget. Like the previous project, Checker's is located in the basement level of an office building, in Philadelphia. The management needed to increase its lunch, "happy-time," and dinner-time draw.

Without endangering the budget, the design team of Dorf Associates were able to add brightness and vitality to the atmosphere. The existing floor and ceiling finishes were retained but the space was reorganized with custom partitions of cherry wood and fluted glass. Stained oak wainscoting and cherry and maple chair rails "add a sense of timelessness and comfort" just as the new sconces and pendant lighting bring "a sophisticated warmth and rhythm to the dining area" that was previously lacking. Other custom touches include the cone-shaped maitre d' stand and the stenciled border at the ceiling perimeter.

Dorf Associates also developed a new logo and graphics package that unifies the design by applying the checkerboard pattern to various elements; silk-screened signage on the storefront glass, waiter/waitress uniforms/menus, napkins, and the inlaid bar top. "This repeated graphics gives Checkers its name, adds a touch of color and whimsy to the palette, and reinforces the identity."

SOHO SOHO

Fifth St., London, England

The concept of this new style restaurant that Virgile & Stone was commissioned to redesign and eventually re-create, is rooted in "the imagery and colors of Provence and the south of France." The two-story restaurant now includes a rotisserie with an open kitchen and a bar on the ground level which can accommodate 150 patrons. A more formal and sophisticated dining ambience for 70 is located on the first level.

The architectural design firm "simplified and rationalized some of the existing elements of the facade" and in doing so they have given an entirely new look to the exterior. All the window frames have been finished in a matte blue/black color and high arches which incorporate light are placed in the front of the building's facade. The signage is also applied to the front in fret-cut, black metal.

Design: Virgile & Stone, London, England
Mural: John Turner

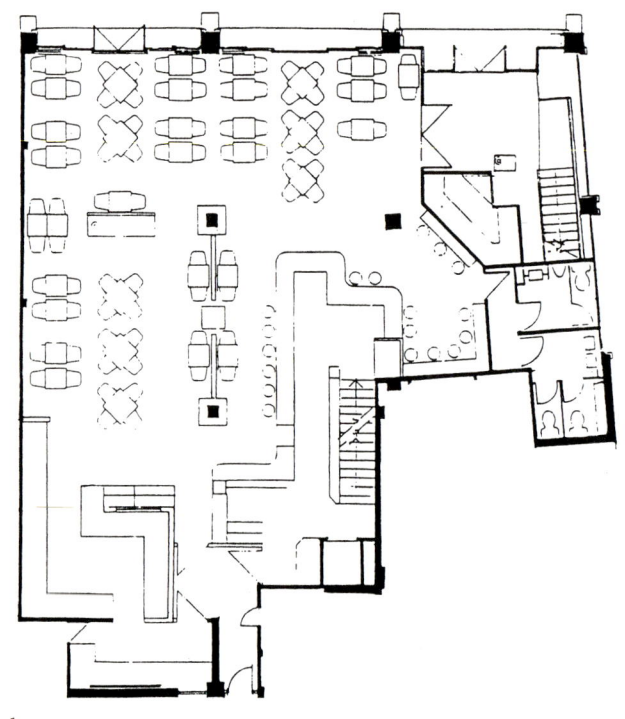

Separating the rotisserie from the bar on the street level are hedges of "growing" lavender plants set into the antique white finished dividers. The floor is laid with large, hand made, baked ceramic tiles, biscuit in color, while the casual, antique white furniture is provincial in styling even to the woven rush seats and the arched ladder backs. They are complemented by the unfinished wood table tops. Surrounding one of the support columns are shelves laden with colorful country-style crockery, herb flavored vinegars and assorted colored oils in glass cruets, plus masses of dried herbs. One long wall is painted a rich, full blue and it is gaily overlaid with white outline figures cavorting a la Matisse.

The "natural sophistication and flavors of the South of France" are captured in the design of Soho Soho by the use of simple devices, finishes, murals, and contrasting textures and colors.

Zoë

Prince St., Soho, New York, NY

Soho, in New York City, is the center for artists and art galleries and it is also the heart of the historical Cast-Iron District with many examples of buildings well over 100 years old. The facade of Zoë consists of folding glass and wood doors while the interior evokes somewhat of a "timeless European atmosphere with such elements as 14 ft. terra cotta columns, original decorative ceramic and mosaic tiles, inlaid stone, and marble details."

The designer/architect was called upon to design a space that would blend a creative American cuisine with the artistic Soho surroundings. The 125-seat restaurant is dominated by the unique open kitchen which includes a wood-burning oven, a large rotisserie grill and 12 seats at the cherry wood counter topped with greenstone — where the action takes place. The rear wall of the kitchen is covered with a rich, sparkling blue/green mosaic of tiles while patterned squares glinting in gold and beige are set into the wall recessed under the terra cotta colored ceiling.

For the walls and colors used in the restaurant, Jeffery Beers took his inspiration from Native American blanket and basket designs as seen on the insets of the kitchen wall. The restaurant walls are sponged and glazed in a yellow to ocher to green-gold ombre which meets the old-fashioned tiled wainscoting below. To this palette, the designer added different marbles, handblown glass from Italy, and cherry wood veneers.

"My primary design challenge was to develop a complementary relationship both visually and functionally between the creative cooking techniques on view and the surrounding environment. At Zoë, the artful presentation of wonderful cuisine is part of the show."

Design: *Jeffery G. Beers, Architects, New York, NY*
Graphic Design: *John Kneapler*
Decorative Painting: *Nancy Kearing/Stefano Loffredo*
Photography: *Paul Warchol*

Bistro 89
Cleveland, OH

Like Zoë, Bistro 89 is also located in a landmarked building — this one is near the water in Cleveland, OH. The owner's, the Strang Corp., wanted a design that would reflect the neighboring lakefront parks and the Gold Coast area of Cleveland. They commissioned G. Herschman of that city to design the 4300 sq. ft. restaurant shown here.

For the 143 seat restaurant, the architect/designer combined the light oak flooring with the deeper mahogany woodwork and separated them with a wainscot of granite tiles. The warm and inviting walls are patina textured to a flattering beige tone and accented with molding strips and feature bands of rubbed copper. The copper topped bar and the service counters echo the same glowing color. Architecturally the designer added soaring, fan topped glazed windows that open up the dining floor to the outdoor patio beyond and he has repeated the curved line in the covered barrel vault of wood overhead and in the shaped copper moldings that accentuate the slightly arced ceiling over the seating area. The custom designed "umbrella"-shaped lamps that hang from the curved ceiling recall the white, square parasols that protect the patio diners from the sun.

This gracious but informal restaurant has become the "in" gathering place and it draws patrons from the nearby downtown business section as well as from the adjacent residential neighborhood.

Design: G. Herschman, Architects, Cleveland, OH

CHEZ GERARD
London, England

Like Soho Soho, in London, this restaurant, Chez Gerard, is also designed by Virgile & Stone. Since most of the older buildings in London are very narrow, retail and dining establishments are often forced to go up or down rather than spread out to the sides. This French-style restaurant is situated on two levels and has a provincial ambience designed to complement the menu.

The architects started with the simple and elegant facade which is now essentially created from pressed zinc, curved glass, and white marble. An etched glass canopy formed from zinc — with two blue canvas side awnings — frames the frontage. The discreet arch lighting element illuminates the sans serif signage.

The small reception area is partially framed by the curved zinc bar which was especially made in France. The wall and ceiling treatment on the ground level is high gloss cream lacquer set against natural wood paneling. Small, off-white ceramic tiles are used to cover the floor. The interior combines banquette seating and small private booths which are separated from each other by etched glass screens. The seating units are upholstered in dark brown leather and cast metal "luggage racks" above the banquette seating can be used to store the patrons coats. They are featured along with bevelled mirrors. Other surfaces and the display shelves are made of honed white marble.

Design: Virgile & Stone, London, England

In the rear there is a more open arrangement of tables and chairs under a glass sky-light roof. This area is also enhanced by a display of wines in a full height cabinet of wood with wire mesh closing doors. Small metal wall mounted lamps add to the warm, intimate atmosphere as do the decorative elements like the zinc pots and the wooden grape trugs filled with wild flowers. The white table china is set off by the subtly colored, checkered cloths.

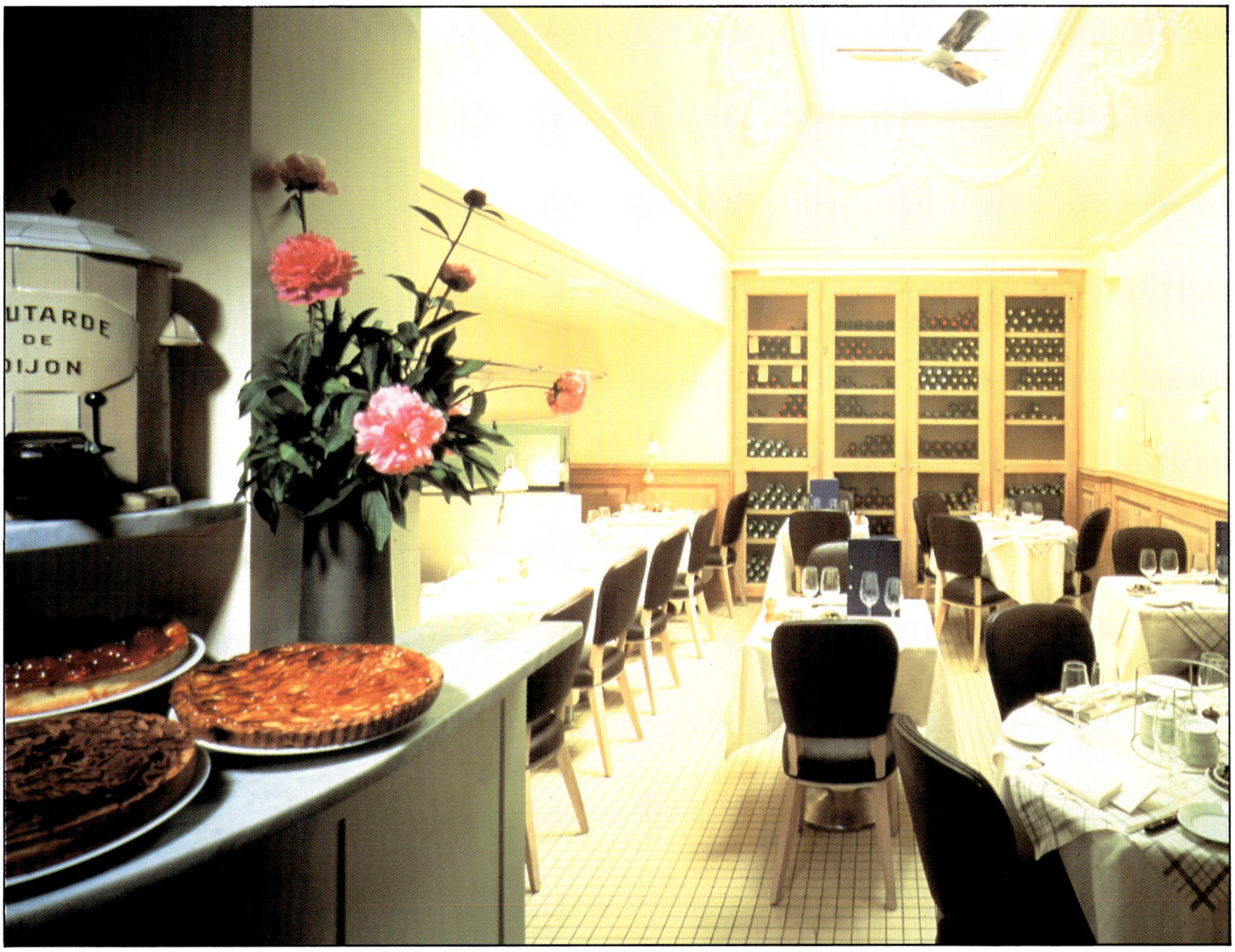
UTARDE
DE
DIJON

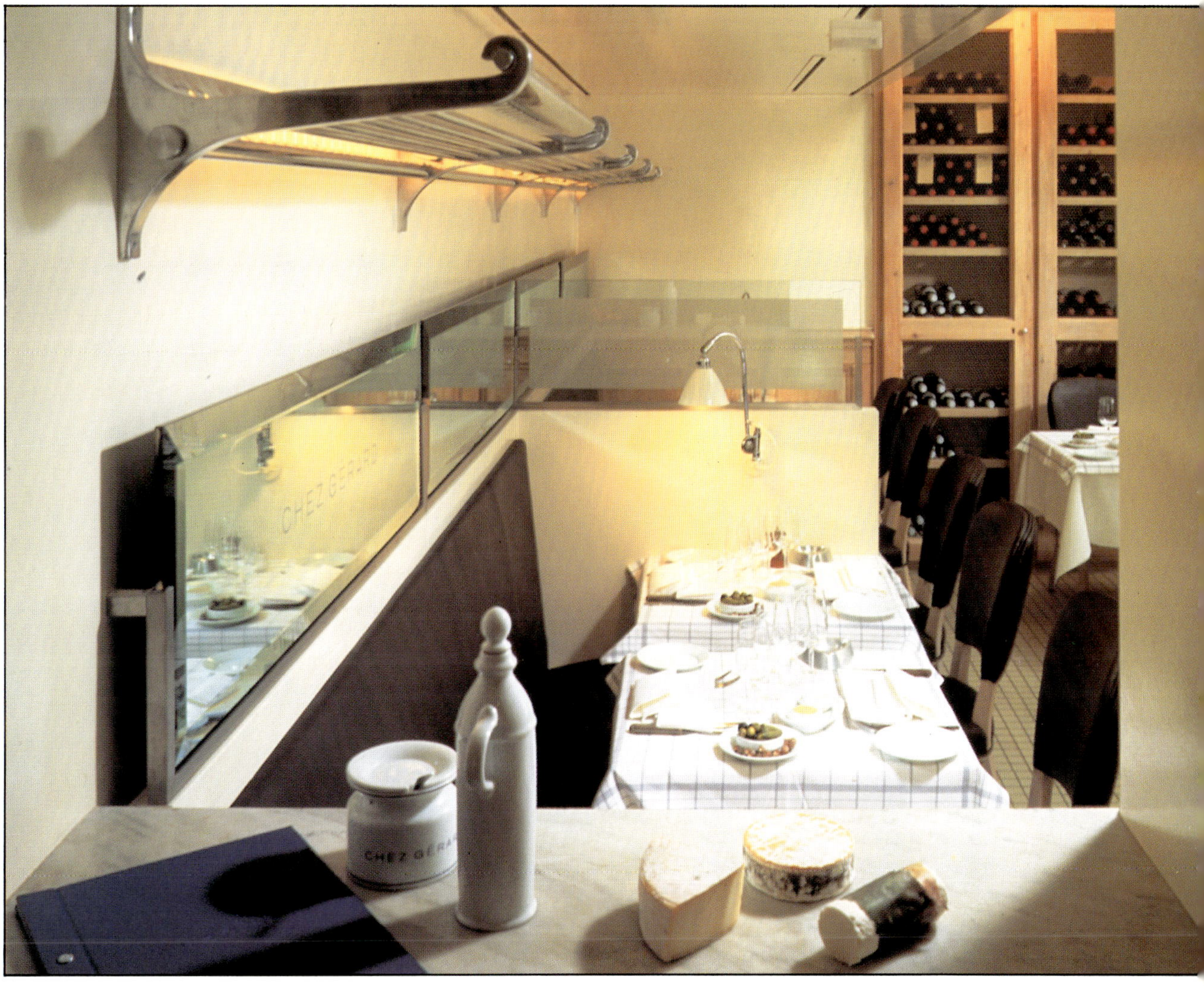
CHEZ GERARD

Morton's of Chicago

Minneapolis, MN

Design: Shea Architects, Minneapolis, MN

Morton's of Chicago is a chain of up-scaled steakhouses which are usually located in the business centers of major metropolitan areas. When the company decided to open a branch in Minneapolis, they called upon the local architectural firm, Shea Architects, to "create a steakhouse in the traditional style" — rich in fine woods, marbles and interesting textures.

An important feature in this kind of operation is the open kitchen so that the diners can enjoy the theater of the assorted toque-topped chefs preparing the individual orders. In this particular Morton's, the open kitchen is the focal point of the warm, wood-floored and low-ceilinged space where the encased mechanical systems are given even greater emphasis by being wrapped in the dark wood veneer. The open kitchen is framed by earthy, pink bricks with glints of copper and decorative ceramic tiles used to outline the serving counter and face the rear wall of the efficient and well lit kitchen.

Beige leather upholstered banquettes hug the perimeter walls while art deco-inspired chairs are pulled up to the tables covered with "traditional" starched white cloths. Displays of wines, fruits and vegetables, and freshly baked rolls in assorted provincial wicker baskets add bright color accents to the otherwise beige/brown palette of Morton's. The rich, glowing incandescent light is designed to make the steaks appear even juicier as they are being served.

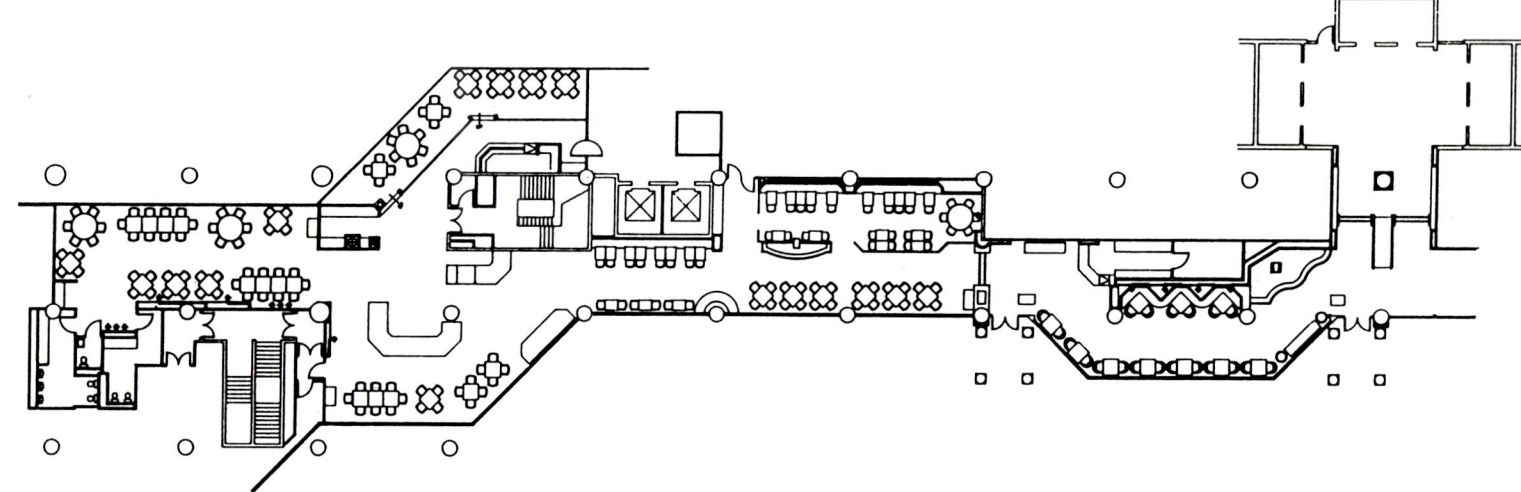

Design: Di Leonardo International, Warwick, RI
Architect: K.N.W. Architects & Engineers, Quarry Bay, Hong Kong
Photographer: Arthur Kan Photographer, Wanchai

Patio Coffee Shop
New World Hotel, Kowloon, Hong Kong

"Bright and colorful" were the words that dominated the design concept for the Patio Coffee Shop which is located on the fourth level of the New World Hotel in Kowloon, Hong Kong. Not only did this restaurant have to be sophisticated to satisfy the up-scale, international visitors who stay here, it also had to be casual and relaxed — pleasantly informal without forsaking any of its elegant character.

Since the view from this space is so important, the designers used no window treatments — the better to let the outdoors come indoors. The patrons actually feel that the courtyard beyond is really part of the coffee shop experience. Food display and the very important open grill were major considerations in the design of this shop. "The food becomes the focal point and we tried to create a background where the people and the food become the environment."

In order to complement the food and the exterior setting — and still keep the interior light and modern, the designers used warm terra cotta colored tiles on the floors and added unusual light fixtures in vivid blue and pink to the otherwise neutral color scheme of off-white and creamy beige.

MI PIACE

Pasadena, CA

In contrast to the ornate exterior of the historic Exchange Building in the Old Town of Pasadena, the Mi Piace Restaurant is quite simple. "It provides a sculptured composition of layered planes and soffits that provide the restaurant with its sculptured identity.

The white walls of the 3000 sq. ft., 90-seat restaurant are punctuated with red sandstone to create an interesting backdrop for the open kitchen and the tempting desserts displayed in glass cases.

A sandstone partition also defines the edge of the bar which is "the centerpiece" of the restaurant. The circular ceiling soffit above the display cases emphasizes the restaurant and separates the dining guests from the newly arrived one. "The bar is conceived as a catalyst; it functions both as a starting point for the restaurant patrons and as an attraction to the newcomers." Working within the small space, Sat Garg, the principal of Akar, the design firm, avoided clutter and instead used rich textural materials, color and lighting to "sculpt the space into a visual composition." From the street, simple glass and steel shelves upon an inclined rift oak wall highlights a few select bottles. Opposite, a large window of colored and textured glass allows a view into the bakery which appeared in the chapter on Markets and Specialty Stores in this book. "The defined openings carefully allow interaction between the spaces creating interest and spreading vitality."

Design: Akar, Inc., Santa Monica, CA
Photographer: John Post

Restaurant
Bar

P
BAKERY

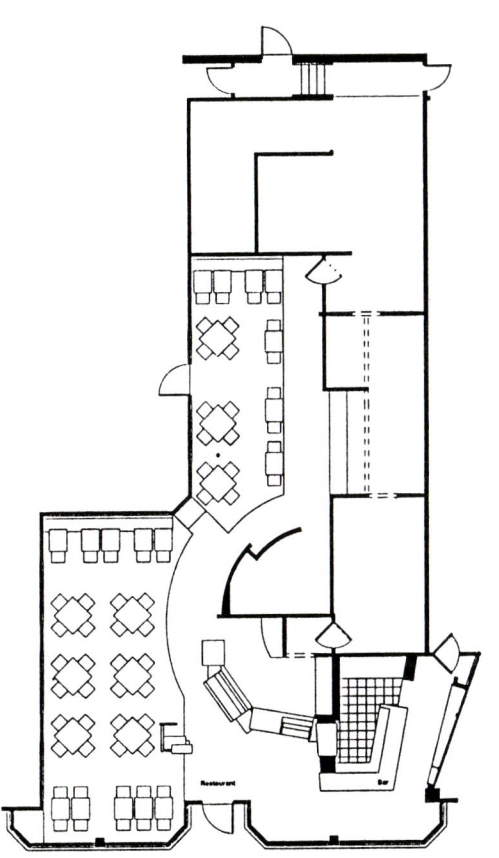

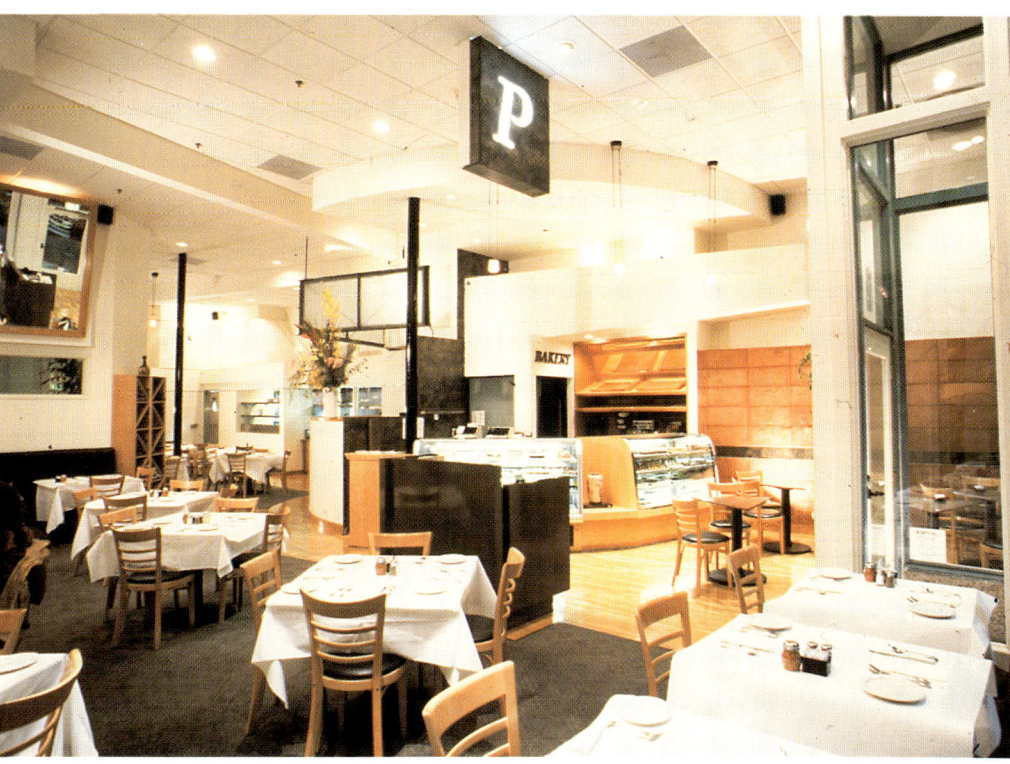

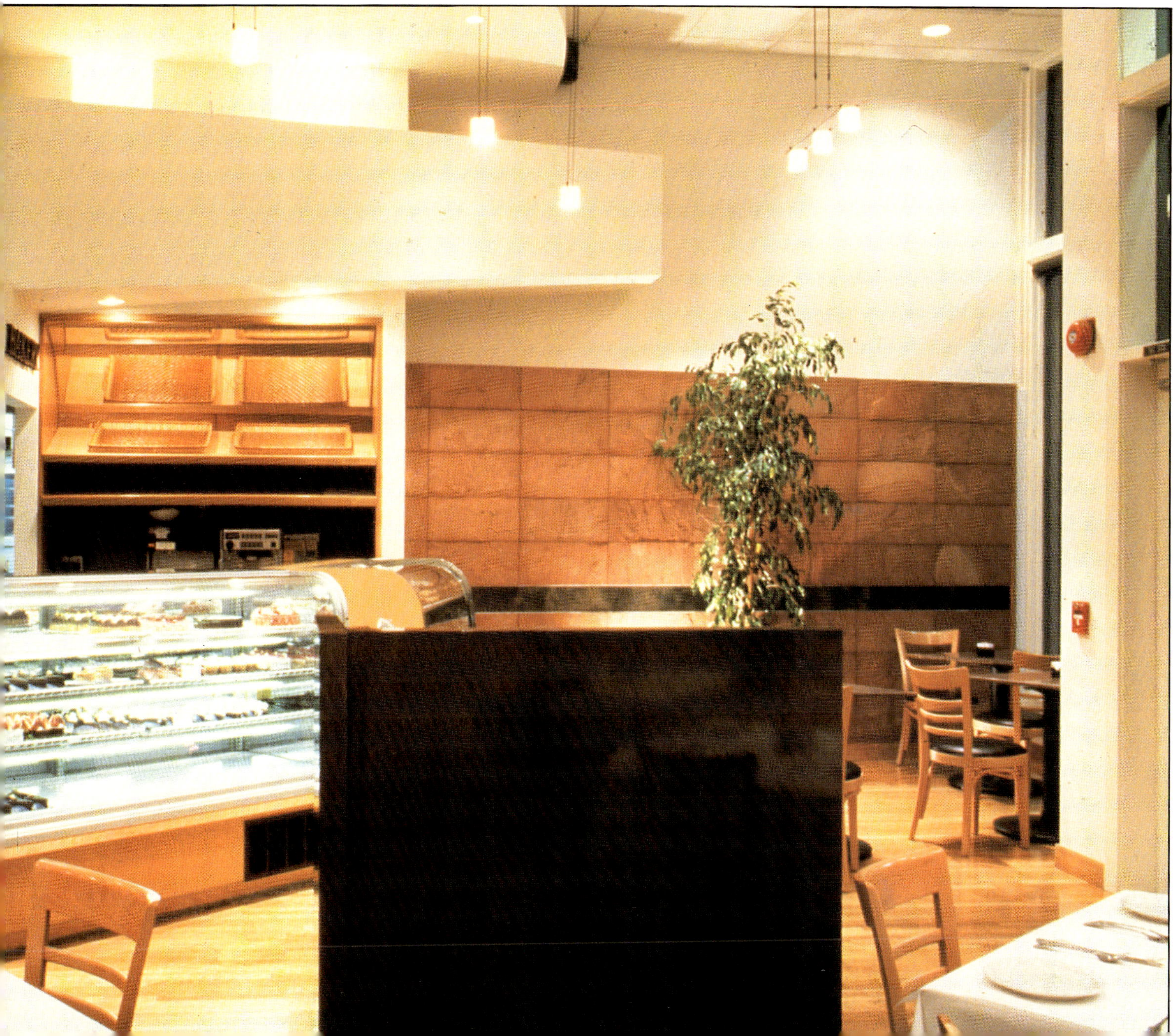

Design: Erkki Jaatinen, Helsinki, Finland
Photographer: Lauri Aitolahti

J.F.F. Kettunen
Konukyla, Helsinki, Finland

The restaurant/pub is subtitled "Just for Fun" on all of its graphics. J.F.F. Kettunen is a chain of informal food facilities found throughout Helsinki and its suburbs and this one is located in Konukyla and can accommodate about 200 patrons in the 460 sq. meter space.

For the Finns, this is a light-hearted approach to casual dining. The pub's colors are somewhat darker and deeper than those of the restaurant area and the designers, Erkki Jaatinen, used lots of woods in finishing and furnishing the space to create the desired informal and relaxed look. The floor is paved with variegated, ocher/gold ceramic tiles and a special "splint and trowel" technique was used to coat and color the walls. Outdoor-type metal street lamps cast a warm glow over the space along with the drop lights and wall applied fixtures.

Rather than add dropped ceilings, the HVAC ducting system is in full view above as it traverses the light-colored ceiling. Plants in large planters add to the indoor/outdoor pub feeling as do the dart boards on the wall, and the other pub games in the space. To add a homey and warm quality, oriental style runners are laid over the hard floors, and colored glass is combined with the decorative moldings and panels of the light painted bar which is the focal point in the pub design.

CAFE UN DEUX TROIS

Foshay Tower, Minneapolis, MN

Cafe Un Deux Trois is a popular New York City bistro in the Times Square area, and for its second location the management selected the towering space in the 1930s landmarked building, Foshay Towers, in downtown Minneapolis.

In what was once a bank, the designers have created a fun, informal dining experience — "a cacophony of materials, fixtures and furniture" that creates a diversity of dining environments.

In this mix and eclectic blend there are rich velvet draperies, bevelled mirrors, crystal chandeliers and deep, upholstered seating in the private dining spaces while on terrazzo floors stand faux painted columns surround faux cloud-painted walls and crumbling plaster walls — also faux painted — and a varied collection of furniture. This hodge-podge is out in the open dining area and bar up front. Anything goes in this setting where diners are invited to draw on the paper-covered tabletops with the colored crayons provided.

"Un Deux Trois challenges and dictates that the experience will be a diverse and engaging environment for socializing."

Design: Shea Architects, Minneapolis, MN

Design: Meisel Associates, Chicago, IL
Construction: Capitol Construction Group, Wheeling, IL
Photographer: Paul Schlismann, Photography

BISTRO 110

Chicago, IL

Bistro 110 is a "casual-style neighborhood bistro and year-round sidewalk cafe" that is located across from Chicago's famous landmark, the Old Water Tower. The specialty of this restaurant is the hearty food that is prepared in the wood burning oven along with pastas, salads, sandwiches and desserts.

The restaurant can seat 135 persons in the dining room, 56 in the cafe, and 25 more at the bar. According to one of the owners, Larry Levy, "A restaurant is like a painting; it is an accumulation of tiny details." The collection of these "details" was left to the noted restaurant design firm of Meisel Associates of Chicago. They followed their client's dictates and made the place look "old but polished — familiar by intriguing." Bistro 110 exudes the charm of a real French bistro since the designers were inspired by L'Ami Louis, in Paris. Here the walnut booths seem to have a patina of age and even the wainscoting has been gently distressed. The room is painted a creamy beige and combined with all of the wood accents, the setting is neutral but warm and inviting.

A large part of the room's success is due to the graphics and artwork of Judy Rifka who seems to have been inspired by the works of Matisse and Chagall. There is an "explosion of color" on the west wall of the restaurant which is entirely devoted to a mural of nudes and fruits and there is a mini-mural on the east wall. The same sort of artwork has been incorporated into the graphics program which includes the menus, match book covers, posters and such.

Challenging the artwork for the diner's attention is the large, wood-burning oven in the kitchen. It is a theater of sorts and diners watch the food going in and coming out of the cavernous stainless steel oven which adds a special flavor to the foods cooked in it.

CHAMPION BREW PUB

Larimer Sq., Denver, CO

In this chapter we have included several informal brew/pub operations and we conclude with this 180-seat, 8000 sq. ft. "micro brewery/restaurant" located in the historic Larimer Square district.

The designers, Semple Brown Roberts of Denver have tried to suggest a turn-of-the-century brewery in this renovation of the basements of two historic old buildings and the construction of a new glass, brick, and steel, two-story structure which had to be compatible with the century-old buildings around it. The new part does have some seating at street level, but the actual full service kitchen, dining area, and sports bar of the Champion Brewery Pub is located in the renovated basements.

Since the majority of the project was constructed below street level, it was "the use of space-expanding illusions, a highly-refined lighting design, and a make-up air ventilation system that turned a formerly dungeon-like atmosphere into a fresh, open space."

Design: Semple Brown Roberts, Denver, CO
Architect: Marc Applebaum
Interior Design: Sarah Semple Brown
Graphics: Marty Gregg, Weber Design Partners
Photography: Andrew Kramer

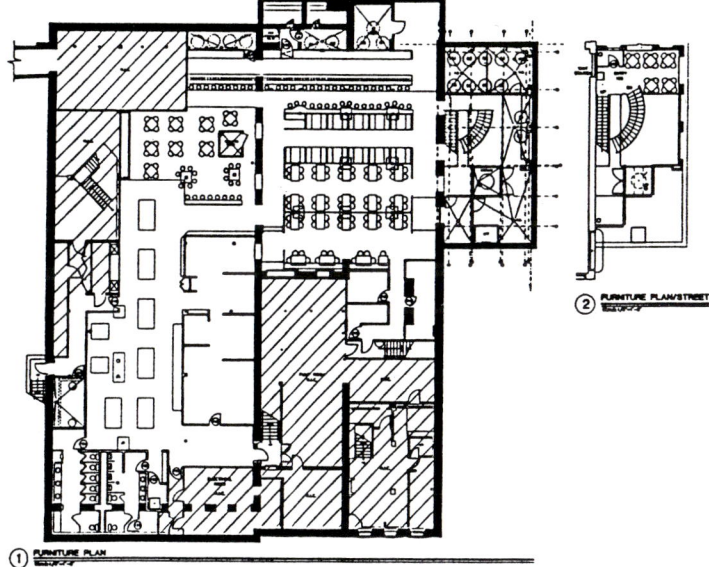

International Flavors & Exhibition Kitchens

Ciao Baby Cucina

Munich, Germany

Ciao Baby Cucina

Washington, DC

Design: Dorf Associates, New York, NY
Principal in Charge: Martin E. Dorf
Photographer: Maseo Ueda Photography

"Food as entertainment" became an important element in this renovation to encourage diners to perceive this space as other than a bar. For the task of re-designing the 7000 sq. ft., 170-seat restaurant, Martin Dorf of Dorf Associates selected a Mediterranean farmhouse vernacular because not only did it reflect the style of the food, it brings with it an image of informality, comfort and warmth. Also, since limited to a budget of $165,000 with which to create a dramatically different store front, bar, and interior — the existing kitchen and restrooms were not involved — the farmhouse suggests millwork and other finishes that are "time-worn, unfinished, inexpensive, and not too time-consuming to produce." Even the expensive mahogany panels of the existing bar and on the perimeter walls of the dining room were resurfaced with 1/2 in. sheet rock which was then finished with faux artwork.

Mahogany cabinetry in the dining room was also resurfaced with #2 common pine and finished with a coat of stain and linseed oil in order to obtain an aged, time-worn surface. The new cabinetry was detailed to allow nail holes and dings and scratches to be visible to further re-inforce the provincial image of a farmhouse. The existing ceiling was painted and 1x6 common pine boards were added to the existing coves. New banquette mirrors were framed with #2 pine frames and also specially made were the crown molding and 14 shelf brackets. The existing carpet was removed to reveal an oak floor which was sanded, stained and sealed with polyurethane while ungauged, multi-colored slate replaced the marble in the bar area.

The owners felt that the restaurant's original "stark, hard-edged image" was too elegant and formal for the menu which is rooted in the diverse history and cultures of the Mediterranean; it draws from the Greek, Spanish, Italian, French, and North African cuisines. The new "Ciao Baby" look has been very effective and more are being planned for other locations.

Tosca

Hingham, MA

The focus of Tosca is a menu featuring Northern Italian cuisine — and wood grilling. The "grilling became the driving force behind both the menu and the design." The design firm, Morris Nathanson Design of Pawtucket, recommended an open kitchen with a full display of the cooking line and food preparation areas — with the spectacle of the wood fired rotisserie and the wood-burning pizza ovens along with the grill as the star attractions. They also recommended full seating at the counter so that customers can "enjoy the excitement of the cooking." In order to accommodate the open kitchen, it was moved to the rear shed area and since the food is prepared almost entirely in the front of the house, the waiters almost never have to enter and disappear into the kitchen.

Tosca is located on Hingham Harbour in an old New England mill that originally serves as a grainery. "Tosca was to become the unexpected — casual, yet sophisticated, dining — much more like Boston." The restaurant formerly located in this space had mezzanine seating which was removed, thus opening up the space to the original wood rafters.

Design: Morris Nathanson Design, Pawtucket, RI
Project Captain: Peter A. Niemitz
Architect: Arris Design Inc., Providence, RI
Photographer: Warren Jagger

These natural supports and the beautiful brick were left exposed and became major elements of the design. A new, custom wood floor — "true to the spirit of the building" — ties the open plan together beautifully. Shards of multi-colored tiles are laid in front of the open kitchen and a warm Tuscan yellow color glows off the rag-rolled walls.

Simple furniture and detailing provide a relaxed ambience to the space. The lighting is kept low-keyed to create a romantic mood.

Lamps appear at tableside to "provide a sense of intimacy at seating height." Adding a touch of theater are the pendant, parchment-shaded lamps over the kitchen and bar, while high hats are used at the ceiling for the overall ambient lighting. To highlight the artwork — old Italian opera posters — there are barn-door spots and the custom chandelier of multi-colored glass "suggests high art."

"Tosca's open place is perfect for people-watching and gives this rather common mill building a warm, exciting, spirited integration of an open kitchen concept that our client's wanted." The total project cost $560,000 for the 5000 sq. ft. restaurant.

Carmine's
New York, NY

The 251-seat restaurant is located on the upper west side of New York City in what was once a red and black vinyl Chinese restaurant with walnut panelling, a hung ceiling, and awful carpeting. The design firm Morris Nathanson Design of Pawtucket, decided to take advantage of the fact that this is a "neighborhood" and so they designed Carmine's as "the quintessential neighborhood restaurant." It is completely fitted to its surroundings and the outside store front and signage blends into the streetscape.

The diner has to walk past a dark, stained black bar with chrome swivel stools with padded vinyl seats to get to the dining room which is located up a half flight of steps. The scale of the dining area is huge and considering that the budget was $200,000 for the job, the designers had to perform design miracles. The hardwood floor that was revealed when the carpet was pulled up was repaired and stained. When the dropped ceiling was demolished, the designers found a wealth of architectural details like grand column capitols, soffits, and moldings — all decoratively detailed. In order to stay within the budget and also keep the homey Italian feeling — "we left the cracks and broken pieces and made no attempt at a clean restoration, but rather made the whole room pull together by painting all the walls a warm and welcoming Tuscan yellow." The terrazzo tiles in a checkerboard pattern in the front entry were restored and polished.

Design: Morris Nathanson Design, Pawtucket, RI
Project Captain: Peter A. Niemitz
Photographer: Peter Paige

"Tables were placed close together and practically touch each other, while their bulging plates full of sumptuous Italian food give off the most incredible aromas! Carmine's is like a movie set; every person's fantasy of a great Italian restaurant. People watching is a key factor here! While it is popular and exciting, Carmine's is still a very relaxed, feel-at-home, kind of place." The lighting fixtures in both the bar and dining room are antiques. They lack conformity and help to establish a sense of fun and interest in the space. Hung on the walls, throughout, are numerous old photographs of "happy Italians" and family celebrations.

MIA TORRE

Sears Tower, Chicago, IL

Mia Torre translates into "my tower" and the 5100 sq. ft. restaurant is located on the restaurant level of the Sears Tower in Chicago. The inspiration for this Italian dining place is the Palio — a 350 year old celebration in Siena that revolves around an unusual horse race. The history, the colorful pageantry, the celebration and the authentic cuisine of Mia Torre "account for the earthy, rich hues of the Siena countryside and the cylindrical tower that is covered with an abstract mural of the Palio flags." Terra cotta, sunflower yellows, rich blues, and deep greens make up the color palette which is the same as is found in Sienese pottery.

A brick-colored floor of tiles runs throughout the space — similar to the cobblestone and bricked square that encompasses the clock tower in the fan-shaped Piazza del Campo — the racetrack for the Palio. Featured in the design is an open-style kitchen which includes a state-of-the-art rotisserie. The main setting is separated from the open display kitchen by a brightly colored, wave-shaped low wall — like a banner being unfurled. Traditional, natural rustic wood chairs and tables are combined with a 15-seat bar, near the entrance, which is also finished in the same rich colors that appear in the dining area. Altogether there is seating for 180 guests.

The graphic logo designed for Mia Torre is a banner with an abstract symbol which was inspired by the emblems that are emblazoned on the flags of the assorted districts or contradas that participated in this annual "medieval pageant/horse race" in Siena.

Design: Meisel Associates, Inc., Chicago, IL
Principal in Charge: Joe Meisel

Azzuro

Upper East Side, New York, NY

Where Carmine's is on the Upper West Side of Manhattan, Azzuro is set on the Upper East Side. Carmine's offers a Northern Italian cuisine, while the Sicloni family-operated restaurant "offers expressive, sun-ripened Sicilian fare."

When viewed through the blue French doors on the sidewalk, the rectangular dining room on view beyond is both formal and casual at the same time. The walls are painted a gentle tan color and the floors are laid with wood parquet squares. Lined up along the walls are numerous antique maps and charts which are framed with the same reddish brown wood used on the floor and on the chairs at the tables. Under a long, framed mirror, there is a high-backed banquette upholstered in a navy and white striped fabric — in keeping with the neutral scheme of the restaurant. Standing lamps with Pompeian red parchment shades add to the warm and cozy ambience of the dining area.

The bar, up front, offers an interesting open wine storage wall and the wood fronted bar is complemented by the natural baked, ceramic tile squares on the floor. A custom Grappa display is suspended from the ceiling which is painted a warm, midnight blue. Sparkling in the summer sky overhead are dozens of recessed lamps that gently illuminate the bar and restaurant areas. As the designers exclaim — "this is a warm, soothing, and comfortable" dining experience.

Design: Tony Chi & Associates, New York, NY
Photographer: Dub Rogers

ECCOLA
Parsippany, NJ

A different look from the same designers of the previous restaurant is Eccola located in Parsippany, NJ. Here, Tony Chi & Associates tried to recapture the essence of what life and romance were like in the post WW II Italy with this "urban courtyard" which brings the past together with today's stylish trends and product presentations.

"Our design is to respond with a new kind of trattoria that is very Italian with none of the cliches — to make an environment palatable to the urbanites." Behind a blue and white, checkerboard tiled serve bar is the open kitchen with its wood burning ovens where individual pizzas can be prepared and offered to bar patrons as late night snacks. Directly in front is a forward bar top of speckled granite which rests on a red mahogany and glass doored crockery cabinet. More of the deep colored woodwork frames the fascia above the open kitchen with cubicles and display shelves for imported cans and bottles of oils, vinegars, wines and other condiments.

A natural, faience baked tile is used on the floor and it is patterned with black tile squares in the walkway in front of the open kitchen. Overhead there are artificial "sky-lights" and centered over the "courtyard" dining area is a raised ceiling filled with floating clouds in a summer blue sky. The "sky" is also pierced with dozens of ambient incandescent lamps that complement the soft glow emanating from the tall, cone-shaded lamps set on the wood dividing wall between the two levels of Eccola.

In the bar area rattan chairs with woven seats and backs are used; stools are pulled up to the curving bar. Patio-style chairs are also set out with the tables on the tiled floor of the "courtyard" under the blue sky.

The designer says, "Today we think of Armani, Versace, and Ferrari — not of checkered cloths and bottles of chianti." This restaurant was designed for Today's diner.

Design: Tony Chi & Associates, New York, NY
Photographer: Dub Rogers

Papa Razzi

Cambridge, MA

Papa Razzi is a popular Italian restaurant located on the corner of a mall in Cambridge, MA — the home of Harvard. The 6000 sq. ft. space has been left quite open and spacious to increase the diner's feeling of being in "a casual, urban Italian restaurant."

The excitement begins on the outside where the bright neon sign is complemented by the fun-colored canvas awnings which were used by the design team to partially hide the facade they were required to work with. Italian tomato can labels are reproduced on some of the awnings for brilliant accents of color — and to add flavor to the exterior. The seating layout, inside, followed the objectives of the client — "to emphasize the people-watching opportunities and to establish a festive dining atmosphere for a variety of seating groups." Some tables are located along the window wall that overlooks the trafficked street and more are set out in the center of the space. The latter are ringed with booths and banquette seating. "The simple wooden chairs and dark upholstered seats, classic banquettes, blade fans, the familiar pendant lights — help to establish the inviting and friendly setting of the neighborhood eating place."

The long mahogany and tile inset bar — to the left of the entrance — can seat another 15 patrons which brings the total seating to 143. The bar flows around and blends into the white tiled service counter that stands in front of the gray and white checkerboard patterned open kitchen filled with stainless steel cooking equipment.

Framed black menu boards overhead add to the friendly and casual spirit of the place. Besides the black lacquered chairs and black upholstery there are many black and white photographs on the walls that re-inforce the black, white and mahogany scheme.

The oak flooring — "straight from the lumber yard" — is stained dark and it is set off by the sand colored coffered ceiling with acoustic tiles. The floor in front of the granite-topped bar is paved with small ceramic tiles laid in an old-fashioned geometric pattern. As a colorful accent, Italian movie posters are displayed along one long wall — in the rear.

The project was completed for $500,000.

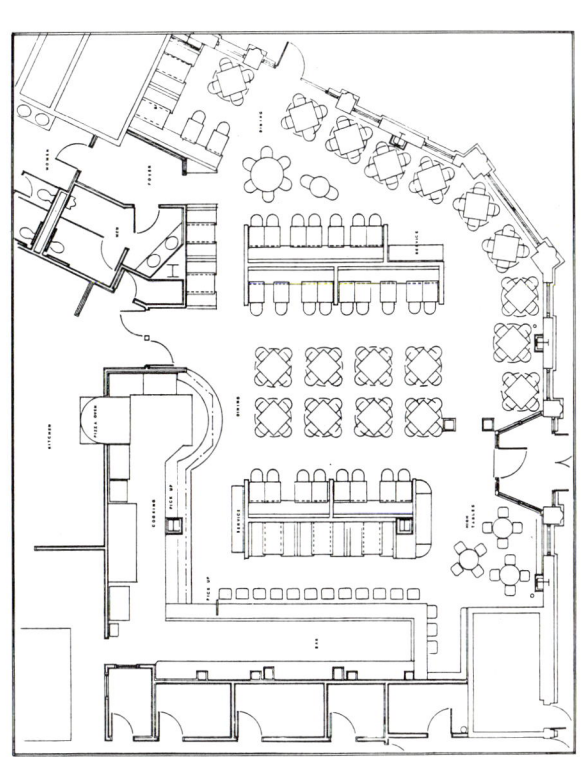

Design: Morris Nathanson Design, Pawtucket, RI
Photographer: Ron Manville

175

Vivo

Chicago, IL

Vivo was the brainchild of the designer/partner, Jerry Kleiner, who together with a businessman, Dan Krasner, and an attorney, Howard Davis, created this Italian restaurant in the Randolf St. market district — amid the warehouses, water-towers and wholesale, produce markets.

In designing the restaurant, Jerry Kleiner relied on the key characteristics of the century-old warehouse; "raw elements were embellished with steel and granite for strength, wood, and pin-spot lighting for softening effects." Patrons entering Vivo are greeted by a magnificent antipasto display atop a massive slab of polished granite. To the left there are thousands of wine bottles stacked on exposed brick walls. The rough-hewn, Italian granite bar runs nearly the length of the right hand side of the space. A twisting metal staircase leads to the vertical shaft which formerly housed the building's freight elevator. Today it accommodates a table for eight in the "most requested perch" in Vivo.

The tables, chairs, and bar stools are hand fabricated of metal and upholstered in assorted colors of leather. The tables are illuminated from the 150, long beam, pin-spots that are positioned up in the 16.5 ft. ceiling.

Design: Kleiner Design, Inc., Chicago, IL
Principal in Charge: Jerry Kleiner

According to the designer, Vivo is "a small, light little room" with only 70 seats. The open kitchen with the wood and charcoal-burning grill shares the wall with the bar. Vivo "is meant to feel like a big living space — like we've asked everyone to come over to our place to eat. That's why the kitchen is exposed — to add to the family feeling" — and to add an enticing aroma to the restaurant's sensual ambience.

BUSKETTI BOY
Fountain Valley, CA

The 1200 sq. ft. space in a strip mall was turned into a new "express" Italian eatery. The intent was to design a whimsical and lively background for the owner's showcase of fresh pastas and pizzas which would appeal to kids and yet be sophisticated enough for the adults to enjoy.

"Angles, curved walls and fixtures were used to carve out a cartoon cityscape of an Italian village." The design team of Hatch Design Group of Costa Mesa, CA used a vibrant palette of yellows, terra cotta reds, deep purples and lapis blues applied with a combed texture — suggestive of strands of spaghetti — to achieve the desired look. Incorporated into the "buildings" are framed windows with vistas onto a "surreal Italian countryside."

The curved cookline counter is made of clear birch and stainless steel and it is faced with purple stained birch panels in an assortment of asymmetrical, angular patterns. The trash enclosures and drink fixtures are framed with deep mottled purple arches of hardened foam. The curved motif of the space is repeated on the red and gold linoleum floor while curlicue door pulls and conical pendant fixtures all add to the whimsy of Busketti Boy.

For other Italian flavored dining ambiences, the reader may want to refer back to the previous chapter on Informal & Thematic Dining to review some of those projects.

Design: Hatch Design Group, Costa Mesa, CA

Design: Sixty First Pl. Architects, Scottsdale, AZ
Principal in Charge: Rafique Islam
Photographer: Don Watts

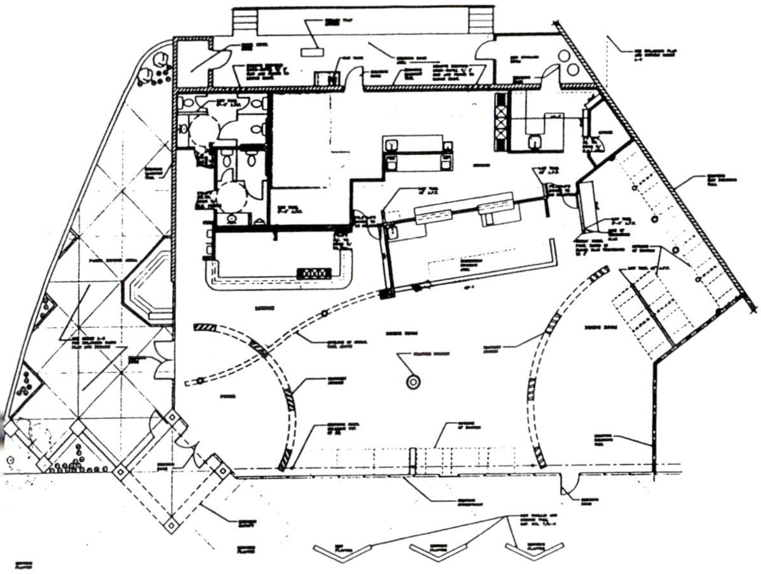

LA PARRILLA SUIZA

Phoenix, AZ

This "Mexico City-Style" restaurant is located in Phoenix, AZ and in addition to the cozy bar and dining in a plaza-like setting, it features an exhibition kitchen where diners can watch tortillas being made — meats searing on the grills, and salsa being prepared.

Two massive curved and arched brick walls transverse the main floor dividing it into smaller and more intimate alcoves and spaces. A large, undulating mural depicting Diego Rivera-inspired pictures of street vendors and dancers in Mexican villages runs from the front lobby to the glistening copper sheathed open kitchen.

The larger dining area is set out under an "open" ceiling filling with twinkling lights and around a monumental column that further enhances the imagery of a Mexican plaza or square. The floor is paved with terra cotta tiles and the wooden table tops are inset with colorful borders of decorated Mexican tiles.

Dos Hermanos

Sears Tower, Chicago, IL

Dos Hermanos, located in the sky-scraping Sears Tower in Chicago, adds to the international flavor of the restaurants in the building with the "authentic, Mexican cuisine served in a straightforward and simple manner." Informality is the basic ingredient here and the authentic Mexican decor and design motifs help to "create the casual warmth" that customers can relax in and enjoy.

Natural wood floors with deep red designs stained on the otherwise clear finish are combined with the natural terra cotta colored tiles in the bar area which along with the open kitchen has seating in red lacquered stools with natural woven rattan seats. Throughout the area is creamy white with textured walls and columns decorated with Mexican hand-painted tiles. A large salad bar makes a tempting statement where all can see it in its tile encrusted case. Colorful Mexican masks and artifacts are freely applied to the light, warm walls.

In addition to the traditional Mexican appetizers and entrees, at reasonable prices, there are margaritas and imported beers. Dos Hermanos also features up-beat and friendly service in this atmospheric and inviting environment.

Design: Meisel and Associates, Inc., Chicago, IL
Principal in Charge: Joe Meisel
Photographer: James Steinkamp, Steinkamp/Ballogg, Chicago, IL

Tres Lobos

Stardust Resort & Casino, Las Vegas, NE

Mexican and continental cuisine is served in this up-scaled restaurant. Tres Lobos is located in the Stardust Resort & Casino in Las Vegas — not too distant from the Forum Shops which was also designed by Dougall Design Associates.

To capture the essence of the two different cuisines, the designer created this quasi-Mediterranean ambience which effectively covers the continental as well as the Mexican specialties of the restaurant. The space is long and narrow and in order to create four separate dining areas, a six ft. wide by 52 ft. long arcaded aisle leads the diner through the space; the courtyard, the patio for informal dining, the more formal dining room and the veranda.

According to Mr. Dougall, the designer, "The guests use the corridor to get to their seats rather than bumping between occupied tables. The colonnade/aisle also serves as the "entertainment area" as it is used by the costumed employees — and people can people-watch from their tables.

A focal point in the design is the fountain at the end of the aisle which consists of three sculptured pineapples backed up by a colorful tiled wall. The designer felt that the tiles added sparkle and pizzazz to the fountain's all-important location.

Rather unique is the illumination of the vaulted arcade/aisle; there are dramatic hanging light fixtures that not only throw light up onto the vaults but also light up the aisle, and set into the marble and slate diagonally-patterned floor are up-lights which further dramatize the architecture.

Design: Dougall Design Associates, Los Angeles, CA

ARCHITECTURAL FLOOR PLAN - LOWER

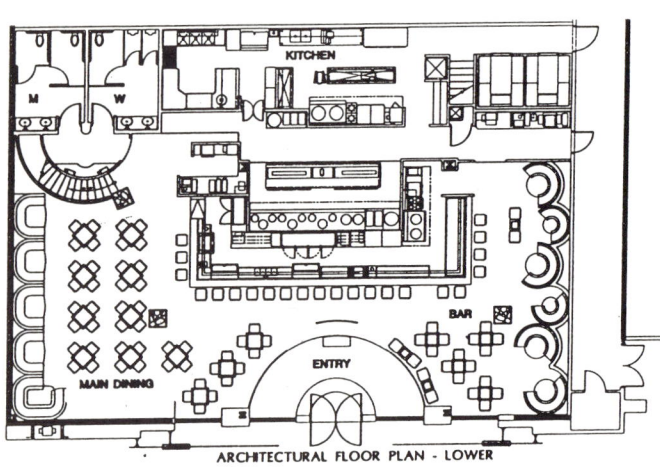

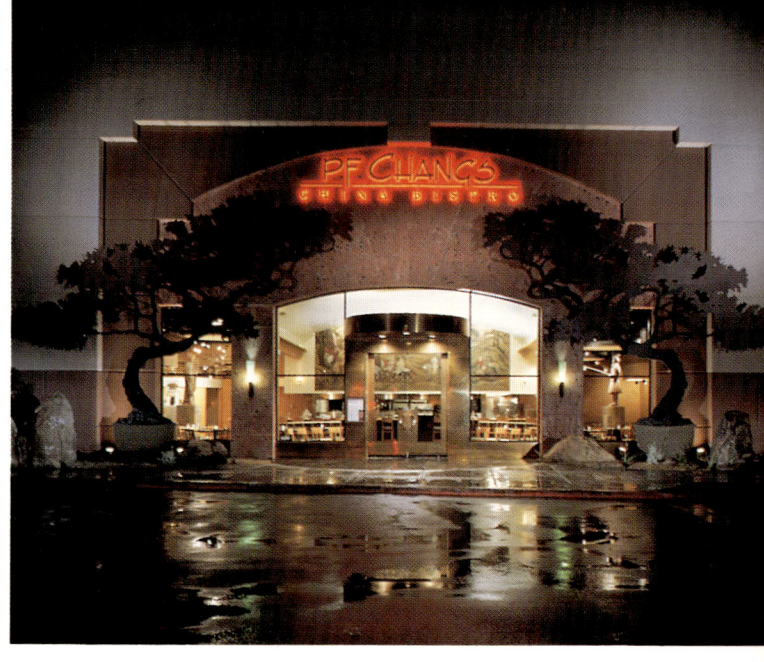

Design: Habitat, Tempe, AZ
Photographer: Mark Boisclair Photography, Inc., Phoenix, AZ

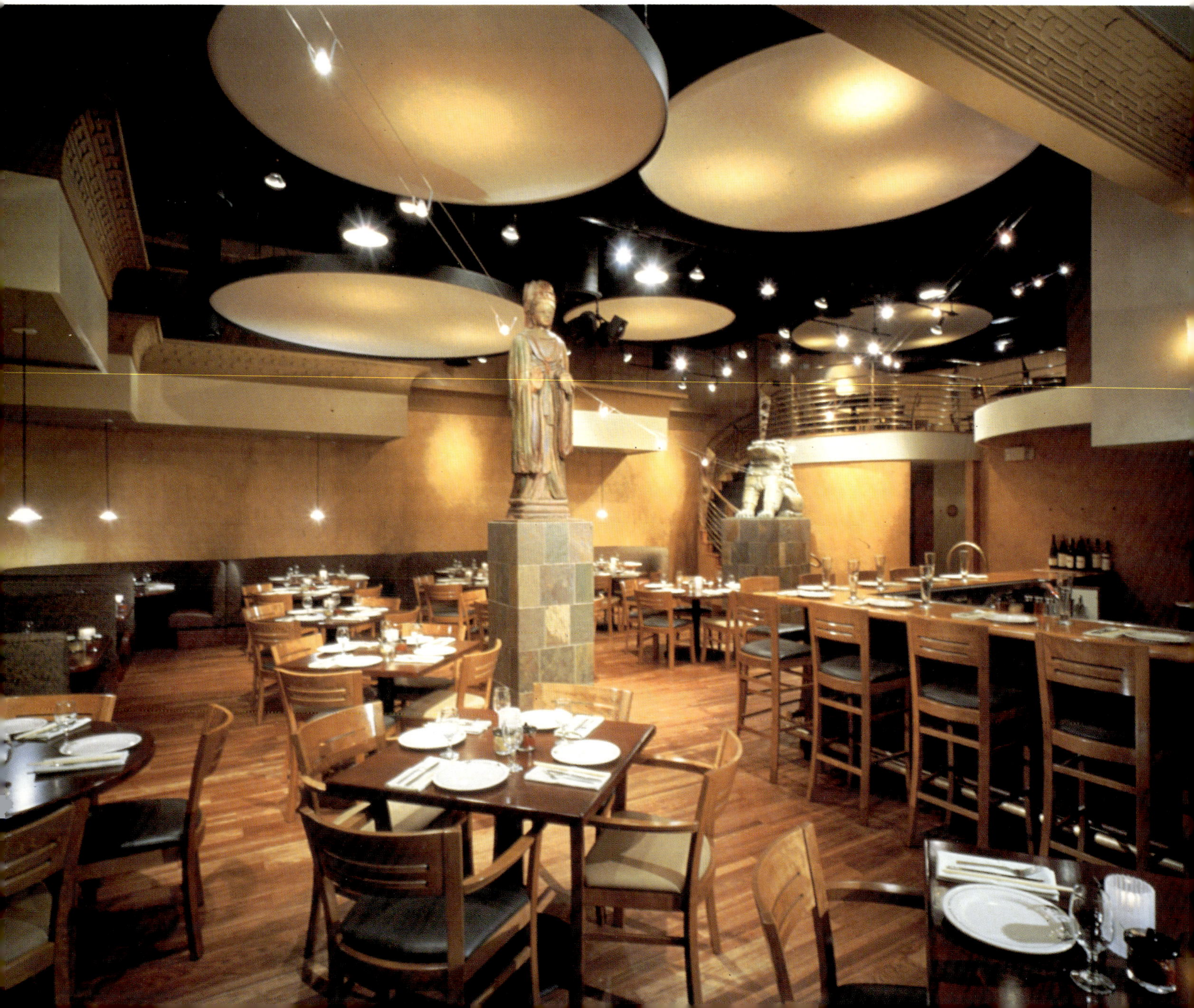

P.F. Chang's

Scottsdale, AZ

The up-scaled, Chinese restaurant is situated on two levels; 4611 sq. ft. on the first level, and 1455 sq. ft. on the mezzanine seating level. The exterior of the restaurant is mainly glass accented with stucco in a "Venetian" palatico finish in terra cotta color.

The patino bronze entry doors are accented with a circular marquis above and metal sills below the windows. Framing each side of the entrance are tree silhouettes, laser cut in intricate detail out of 1/4 in. steel plate. Large boulders and an Oriental-style garden is another exterior attraction of P.F. Chang's whose name appears in neon, back-lit, patino bronze letters.

The centerpiece of the interior is a 26 x 10 ft. mural which rises above the exhibition kitchen area. The see-through kitchen is set behind a bar that can accommodate 21 patrons for an un-ending show.

The interior design and architecture, affected by Habitat of Tempe, AZ, combines a palette of bronze, mustard, purple, and black with textured surface materials like wood, metal, and stone. In the design and decor there is "a contemporary application with hints of Chinese symbolism."

One of the major problems the designers faced was in effectively re-routing all the mechanical systems, exhaust, make-up air, pipes and vents which had to be led horizontally to and then through the exterior wall and then vertically raised in shafts 45 ft. up to the roof of the building.

Tang's Ginger Cafe

Minneapolis, MN

The client approached Shea Architects with a list of requirements, and an extremely limited budget. Tang's Ginger Cafe was to be an American-Oriental cafe serving Oriental cuisine with a full service wine bar, dining area, and take-out station.

The designers unified the four unique advantages that the restaurant would offer; theater kitchen, pride in food and desire to display, an existing curved corner and a wine bar/take-out. They then defined each by creating a focal point for each asset. All of these are organized and displayed panoramically — "as the entry vestibule sequentially frames and directs views and flow." A tiled, graphic soffit acts as a "corrective spline piercing the space diagonally and gathering pieces into a unified whole." Oriental references are made with logo/graphics reminiscent of Oriental scrip, pagoda-like furniture selections, and wok-like lighting fixtures.

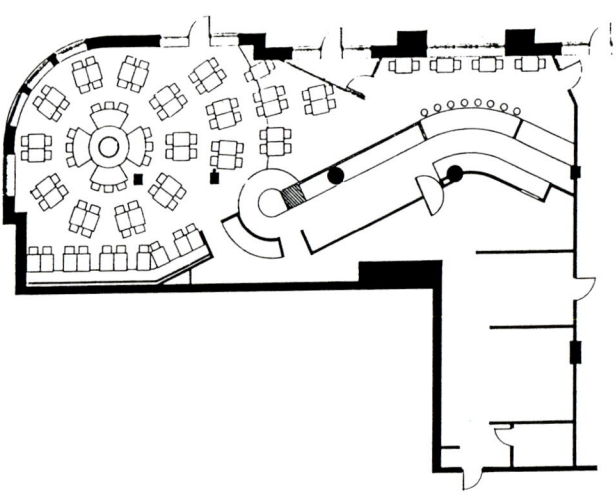

The low budget necessitated simplicity and innovations like the aniline-dyed concrete floor, wall sconces with common light bulbs hung behind mirrored screens, sleeved bolts as coat hooks, entry light poles made of hollow metal pipe stock and a nylon fabric ceiling element that re-inforces the geometry of the space and also provides a sense of scale. The maitre d's stand is also light and portable.

The cafe's name is tied to the design with the placement of a symbolic ginger plant/light sculpture/banquet at the circle center-most "which becomes the organizer for the dining room and the symbolic and visual focus for the entire cafe."

Design: Shea Architects, Minneapolis, MN

Ollie's

Upper West Side, New York, NY

"Working with a modest budget, we knew we did not want a typical red formica Chinese interior, but rather a more uptown concept." The designers, Morris Nathanson Design, realized that the interior had to cater to the neighborhood cross-section on-the-go, and also handle an all-important take-out business.

Ollie's is located on Broadway, on the Upper West Side in New York City in a culturally-diverse neighborhood that is also becoming a fashionable shopping area. "We began by opening up the front of the restaurant to the outside as we wanted little interruption between the interior and exterior." Plate glass framed only by glass block pilasters creates an uninterrupted view to passersby — and to diners alike. An open display kitchen was designed to offer maximum food display and prep cooking. Hanging against the exhibition kitchen's wall are poultry, vegetables, and cooking utensils which, along with the swift and deft movements of the cooks, add to the entertainment and excitement at Ollie's.

The food counter and open kitchen stretch almost the full length of the restaurant and "works as a unifying element." Rippled glass framed in aluminum serve as section dividers and also separates the diners from the cooking area, without interfering with the visibility. The restaurant can seat 112 diners.

The colors of Ollie's are predominantly warm, golden tones which appear on the walls, on the tiles, and in the oak and pine furniture used. "This gives a light and uplifting effect to the interior." In addition to the menu there are some select Oriental artworks hung on the walls that help to suggest that this is a sophisticated Chinese restaurant. The total construction cost — not including the kitchen equipment — was $225,000.

Design: Morris Nathanson Design, Pawtucket, RI
Photographer: Warren Jagger

Panorama

New World Hotel, Kowloon, Hong Kong

Framed by 20 ft. floor-to-ceiling windows is a dazzling harbor view of Hong Kong as seen from Panorama, a sea-food dining restaurant atop the new New World Hotel in Kowloon. To the left of the breathtaking vista is an equally beautiful presentation — of the daily catch items and a glassed in case of over 100 bottles of wine.

A few steps beyond the lounge area is the long, narrow dining room where the 28 tables have been arranged for "casual privacy" along with the aforementioned view — and the goldfish swimming about in centerpieces on each table. Panorama was designed by Di Leonardo International of Warwick, RI in warm and gentle neutral tones as the perfect setting for the stark white china on which the elaborate food preparations are presented. The Swiss artist, Susi Kramer, used vivid colors and abstract shapes to create the "show-stopping, show-plates."

Natural woods glow under the warm incandescent light in Panorama, and the light level is kept romantically low keyed so as not to compete with the spectacular light show reflected in the water of the harbor below.

Designer: Di Leonardo International, Warwick, RI

Clay Pit

Chapman Market, Los Angeles, CA

The Chapman Market complex during its heyday — in the 1920s — served the middle class of Los Angeles with its produce and food market. The complex has a spacious courtyard and a unique blend of Gothic and Spanish architecture.

The Clay Pit was designed by Akar of Santa Monica as "a courtyard restaurant" — "designed to maintain a constant dialogue between the inside and the outside." It is located in a long, narrow 1500 sq. ft. space in the one-story part of the building and it is only 16 ft. wide. The restaurant design has virtually left intact the open wood-truss ceiling and the pressed concrete floors of the original architecture. The focal point is the glass enclosed "open area" where the bread baking process is carried on in view of all of the diners.

The front counter is made of poured concrete and has an integral color finish. It serves to separate the dining room from the open kitchen. An adjoining wall is "rendered with adobe stucco — to resonate the surrounding California vernacular." Complementing the layout of the space are hanging spatulas and strainers that provide the "art" for the restaurant.

Design: Akar, Santa Monica, CA
Design Team: Sat Garg & Venki Blyberg
Photographer: John Post

KIN KHAO

Spring St., New York, NY

"Kin Khao literally translates to 'eat rice' in the Thai language, but the phrase embodies the larger spirit of Bon Apetite — warm welcome and good health." Brad Kelley, the restaurateur wanted a place that would be as indigenous to Bangkok as to New York — not like the usual oriental restaurants where the diner often feels incidental to the gaudy finishes on the walls. Bogdanow and Associates came up with a design in which "diners are as essential as the surroundings" and the design grew out of the extensive research of market-style restaurants in Thailand.

The finished space focuses on the open kitchen "as a stage complete with fire, smoke, spice, and drama." It is contained on two sides by an eating bar which encourages single patrons to enjoy the culinary spectacle. Across from the kitchen, the bar completes the axis around which all activity revolves in Kin Khao. "As the kitchen is the essence of the Orient, the bar is the essence of the Occident." The oak and mahogany bar was found in a cellar somewhere in Staten Island, and it was re-assembled with love and care. Today, it adds a turn-of-the-century tavern charm to this space with its ornate carvings and bevelled mirror trim.

Design: L. Bogdanow Associates Architects, New York, NY

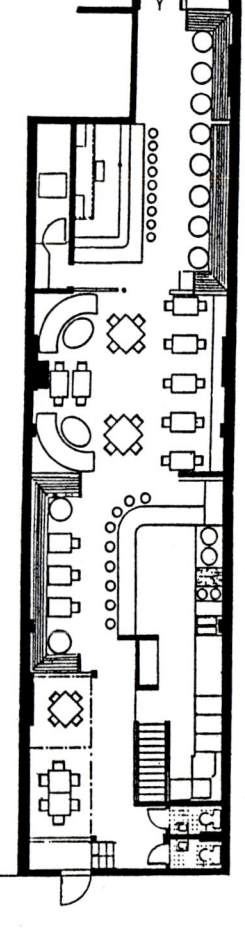

Table patrons sit on simple chairs or hand crafted wood benches which are at once rustic and formal. "This contrast is also echoed in the gnarled tree trunks which define the corners of the distinct dining spaces which are screened with finely finished wood details and draped with fabrics.

"Kin Khao bespeaks the welcome, warmth, and honesty of the ingredients in both its cooking and its architecture." The 2000 sq. ft. restaurant was completed at $75 per sq. ft.

VONG

Third Ave., New York, NY

A completely different look in Thai dining. The design firm of Haverson Rockwell of New York was asked to create an elegant, up-scaled dining environment in Philip Johnson's pink granite "Lipstick Building" on Third Ave. which would complement the Thai cuisine done with a French twist.

The diner enters through the red stained mahogany doors into the bar and lounge area which is dominated by the red stained, pear wood bar inlaid with distressed copper panels. The bar curves sinuously as does the back bar behind it and continues into the dining area of Vong. The straight wall, opposite the curved one that is the passageway from the bar to the dining room is composed of a golden collage of stamps, wallpaper, currency, and artifacts that tell an intriguing story. A series of floor mounted mahogany fans "inspired by mysterious and exotic oriental spaces" accent the wall.

Design: Haverson Rockwell Architects, New York, NY

In the main dining room Thai architectural elements appear in the form of carefully-placed set pieces. The tatami platform recalls the traditional furnishings of Thai country houses and a private party can be seated here — or several couples can share the one long table. One specialty booth is framed by a curved mosaic encrusted screen that recalls a Thai temple and another booth is framed by a scroll edge screen around a distinct opening.

"The kitchen entrance is a metaphor for a sacred portal which is fitting given Vong's special cuisine." A gold leafed ceiling and corresponding textured walls are given a "mystical glow" by the randomly-placed, blow glass lighting textures that are reminiscent of the Thai "festival of lights." Dark stained Brazilian cherry flooring is used to set off the golden eminence of the elegant space.

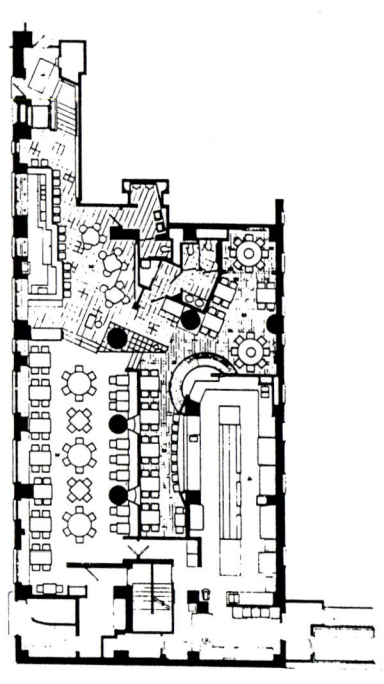

Design: Meisel and Associates, Inc., Chicago, IL
Principal in Charge: Joe Meisel

EURASIA
Chicago, IL

For reasons of economy, the original kitchen and bar locations were maintained by Meisel & Associates, the designers, when they undertook the design assignment of transforming the narrow, low ceilinged space into a lively, contemporary dining environment — where East and West comingle.

First and foremost was to increase the actual — and the apparent space. A new dining room was created when the existing toilets were relocated and this space can be closed off by using custom painted screens patterned after a traditional Japanese firecoat. Visually, the dining room was expanded by opening up the kitchen wall and by providing additional counter seats which view the action inside and display kitchen. Boarded-up windows, on the opposite wall, were opened up to create "a show window back bar" which expands the dining area out into the street. A long shelf of Chinese slate is accented with a variety of Noguchi acari lanterns which "provide a soft glow inside and an intriguing presence from the outside."

Oriental textures, materials and colors were used to provide a background for an art collection tailored for this project. Granite pavers and a cocoa mat at the entry lead to an "abstract garden of tile stepping stones on the bar." A custom-designed carpet — suggestive of the traditional straw tatami mat is used in the main dining room and it is complemented by the match stick birch floor in the raised dining area. Bamboo tan walls provide a background for the jade green columns. The spade is indirectly lit by a rice paper shoji screen used as a ceiling reflector.

CAFE PACIFICA

San Francisco, CA

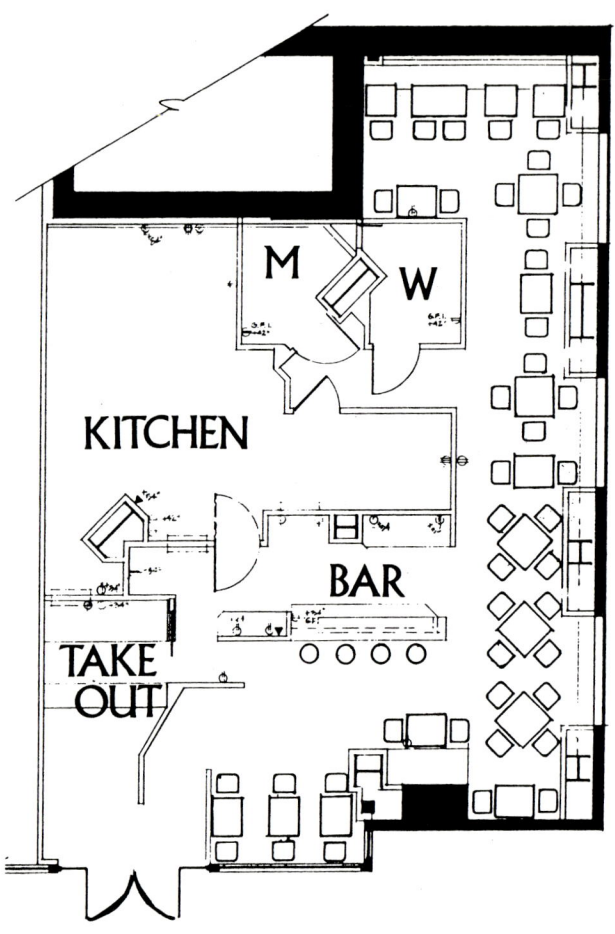

Kozo Iwamoto, the owner of Cafe Pacifica, wanted his restaurant to look contemporary and not have the usual design elements used in Japanese sushi bars and restaurants. "Cafe Pacifica is a new concept in the sense that it serves Dim Sum in the tradition of Japan which has taken the traditional Chinese Dim Sum specialty one step farther by using fresh ingredients, faster cooking preparation and lighter oils." The dishes are prepared in the Japanese-style of arrangement and simplicity.

Located in the ground space of a granite super high-rise building in the financial district, Calvin Lau, the designer, managed to create a comfortable, light and airy, casual dining space. The seating is contemporary in styling and upholstered with fabrics that complement the carpet. The sloped ceiling, the soft peach colored walls, the art niches in the columns, and the wall sconces all blend to highlight the height of the space and yet create a sense of intimacy. Though there are some noteworthy furniture pieces such as antique Chinese altar tables, screens and paintings, the restaurant is unmistakably Japanese in feeling.

The small bar for "take-out is made of simple woods with an ebony finish. The bar top and table tops are laminated with custom oxidized copper plates with swirling, cloud-like, colors. Like the food — Cafe Pacifica is another example of East meets West — and go together.

Design: Calvin Lau Design, San Francisco, CA
Photographer: Michael Lewis

Honmura-An

Soho, New York, NY

Honmura-An is the third restaurant for this authentic noodle shop that even boasts of one that is 65 years old and still thriving in Tokyo. Soba is the main dish; a buckwheat noodle that is the original Japanese "fast food." It is slurped by workers on the go and is usually mixed with combinations of meat, fish, and broths.

Design: Richard Bloch, Architects, New York, NY
Photographer: Tom Reiss, New York, NY

The third generation restaurateur, Koichi Jun Kobari opened this glorified "Sobaya" (noodle shop) in the Soho area of New York City. He says, "Soho is full of artists and galleries and very sophisticated, well-traveled, health-conscious people who are willing to try something new." The space is located on the second level of a landmarked, cast iron building and the designer, Richard Bloch, designed a "shell" for Kobari to embellish as he pleases. The kitchen was designed by the Japanese architect Yasuda Sensei who did both of the Tokyo sobayas and Kobari's friends, some of whom run galleries in San Francisco, contributed many of the artist designed objects that enhance the simple "shell." What Bloch did create was a space that incorporates rich, natural materials such as aged brick, cherry wood, pale green limestone, and panels and elements of satin rubbed steel. Kobari feels that these materials do relate to Japanese design — "but the space can include contemporary elements as well."

Bloch based his seating plan on the Bistro concept which means flexible seating arrangements of tables and chairs combined with banquettes — all of which can be added to or subtracted from — or re-arranged — depending upon the desired circulation or the diner needs. A U-shaped family table is the only big piece in the scheme and it is fashioned after the ones in Japan and used for groups.

From this vantage point, the diners can see the glass and rubbed steel "hut" where the soba chefs are at work on unfinished white cypress tables rolling and cutting the soba. "Watching the process shows you that everything is very labor-intensive and done by hand."

The original brick wall had to be sanded and sealed and some of the steel girders were purposely placed in an asymmetrical arrangement to disguise some of the mechanical containers. The floors were finished with cherry wood and they seem to unify the large space.

Sony Sushi Club

Sony Building, New York, NY

The 17 x 20 ft., five-seat sushi restaurant is as exclusive as it gets. It is located on the 35th floor of the Sony Bldg. on Madison Ave. and E. 56th St. — formerly the AT&T building designed by Philip Johnson. "An astringent, evocative design but not literally Japanese look was sought. Sound and smell were among the senses that we were to serve."

All components of this special, jewel-like restaurant were custom designed and they include the special lacquered panels from Japan, cotton fabrics from India, green limestone, totami mats, etched glass, handmade cedar wood cabinets, a custom, flush-with-the-counter top "neta" (fish display) case and a narrow steam that flows past gilded and block rocks that separates the chef from each guest. Since each of the five guests is "special," each seat has its own, individual colored seat. The sushi club was designed especially for Barry Wine, the V.P. of Sony Club who was previously the chef and owner of the Quilted Giraffe and so allusions and artifacts from that famous dining spot have been included here including the bowed granite bar which was "filched" from the now defunct operation.

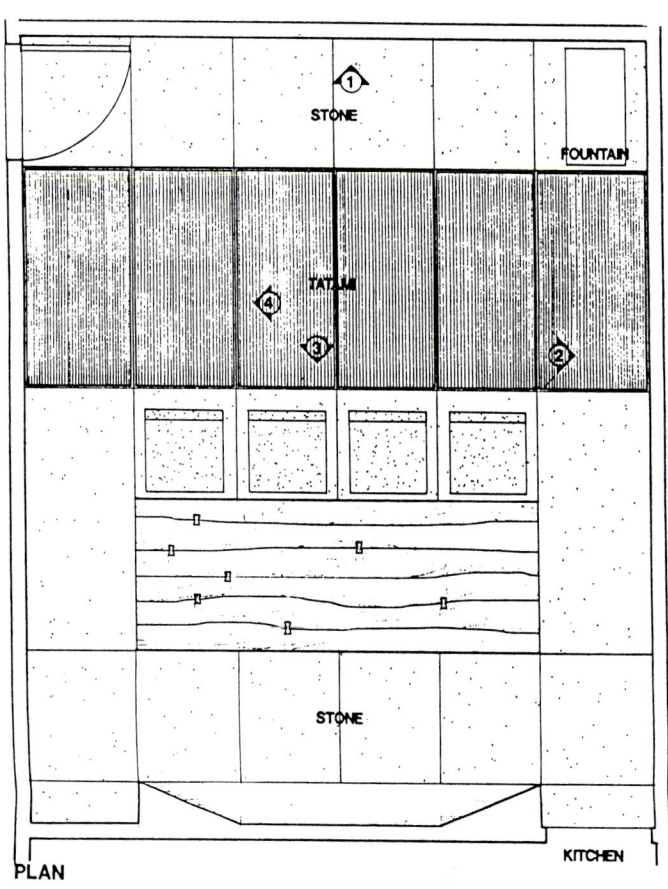

Design: Yuibloch Design, New York, NY
Principals: Jim Yui & Richard Bloch
Photographer: Tom Reiss

Food Courts
& Fast Food
Concessions

STATE FARE FOOD COURT
Gaviidae II, Minneapolis, MN

STATE FARE FOOD COURT

Gaviidae II, Minneapolis, MN

Gaviidae II is one of the two elegant, in-town, vertical shopping centers in downtown Minneapolis, and located on the very top floor is this wonderfully-exciting and exuberant flash of lighting and splashes of color and a keen sense of whimsy that make the State Fare Food Court so unique.

Designed by the Minneapolis design firm, Shea Architects, the theme is based on the Minnesota State Fair and "through the use of lighting, color, materials, motion, and detail," they have tried to "evoke the imagery, history, and magic of the State Fair experience within an up-scaled, retail environment." Flashing marquee lights, polychromatic fluorescent lights, strobing neon and canvas awnings provide a canopy above eye level for the giant, over-scaled and fantasy-land versions of hot dogs, ice cream cones, peanuts, corn on the cob, and french fries — all turned into three-dimensional column covers over the actual supporting members of the floor. The black and white terrazzo floor is patterned with sweeping curves and sharp angular lines to continue the same sense of excitement below. The tables in the seating area are red, or yellow laminates or black and white photos of old-time fair scenes enlarged and embedded under coats of polyurethane. Illuminated arcades and murals of fair scenes complete the range of sights and smells of "our State Fare."

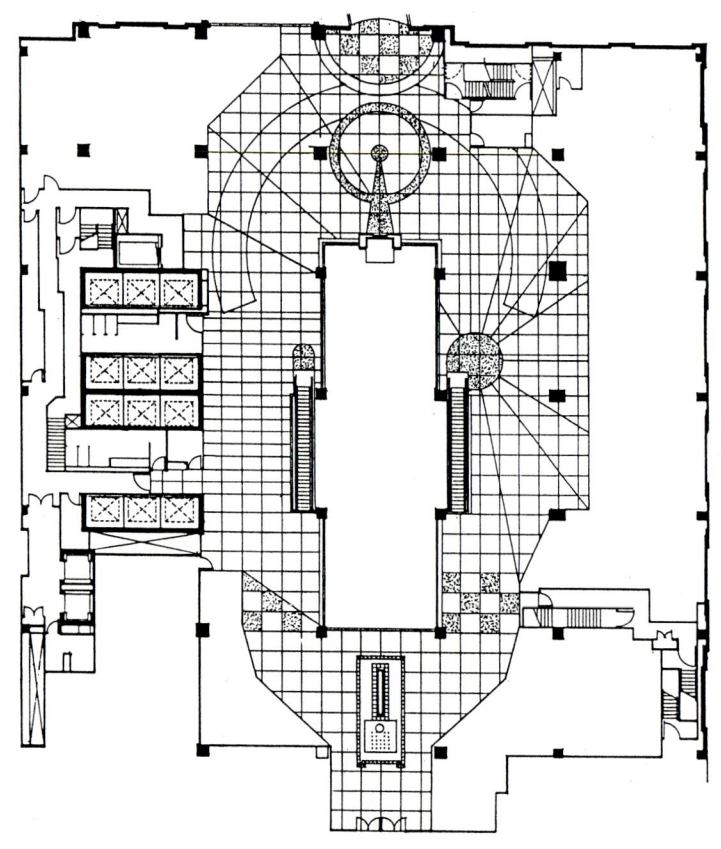

Design: Shea Architects, Minneapolis, MN
Photographer: C.M. Korab / MMP/RVC

MALL OF AMERICA FOOD COURTS
Bloomington, MN

Located in Bloomington, MN — just a few minutes away from downtown Minneapolis — and surrounded by large regional malls on all sides is the new mega-mall. Though it is not the largest mall in the world, The Mall of America is the "largest fully-enclosed combination retail and family entertainment complex in the U.S." The hyper-construction is located on the 78 acre former site of the Metropolitan Stadium and of the total 4.2 million sq. ft., 2.5 million is devoted to retail space.

On the top story of North Garden — one of the four sides of the mall is one of the two major food courts that serve the visitors to the Mall of America. Some of the names of the food tenants are familiar to mall goers anywhere across the U.S., but others are quite new. The space that is devoted to the food court is generous — all spread out under the wide expanse of skylights that provide an optimal amount of daylight. To continue the "village/garden theme of the North Garden, there are terra cotta pots overflowing with greenery attached to the many light colored columns that support the high tech ceiling above. Bright and sunny yellow umbrellas top some of the garden type tables, and chairs provided for the diners convenience.

From here the diners can enjoy a view of Camp Snoopy in the open atrium just alongside the food court or watch the would-be golfers lining up to play the multi-leveled gold course. Way over on the other side of sprawling Camp Snoopy in the more up-scaled part of the mall, South Avenue, is another food court. This one is colored peach/rose, soft green, and gray. Here the coloring is rosier and gentler, and the ambience includes old-fashioned "gas" lamps, trees in planters, and the sunbrellas in pastel rose and green sprouting out over the dining tables — all under the truss and glass ceiling. In addition to the Chinese, Japanese, Mexican, Italian, and other international, taste satisfying concessions, there are some that are uniquely "local." See the next pages for some of the food stands in the Mall of America.

Architects: Hammel Green Arbrahamson, Inc.
Korunsky Kron Ericson, Minneapolis, MN
Graphic Design: Kiko Obato & Co., St. Louis, MO
Photography: MMP/RVC

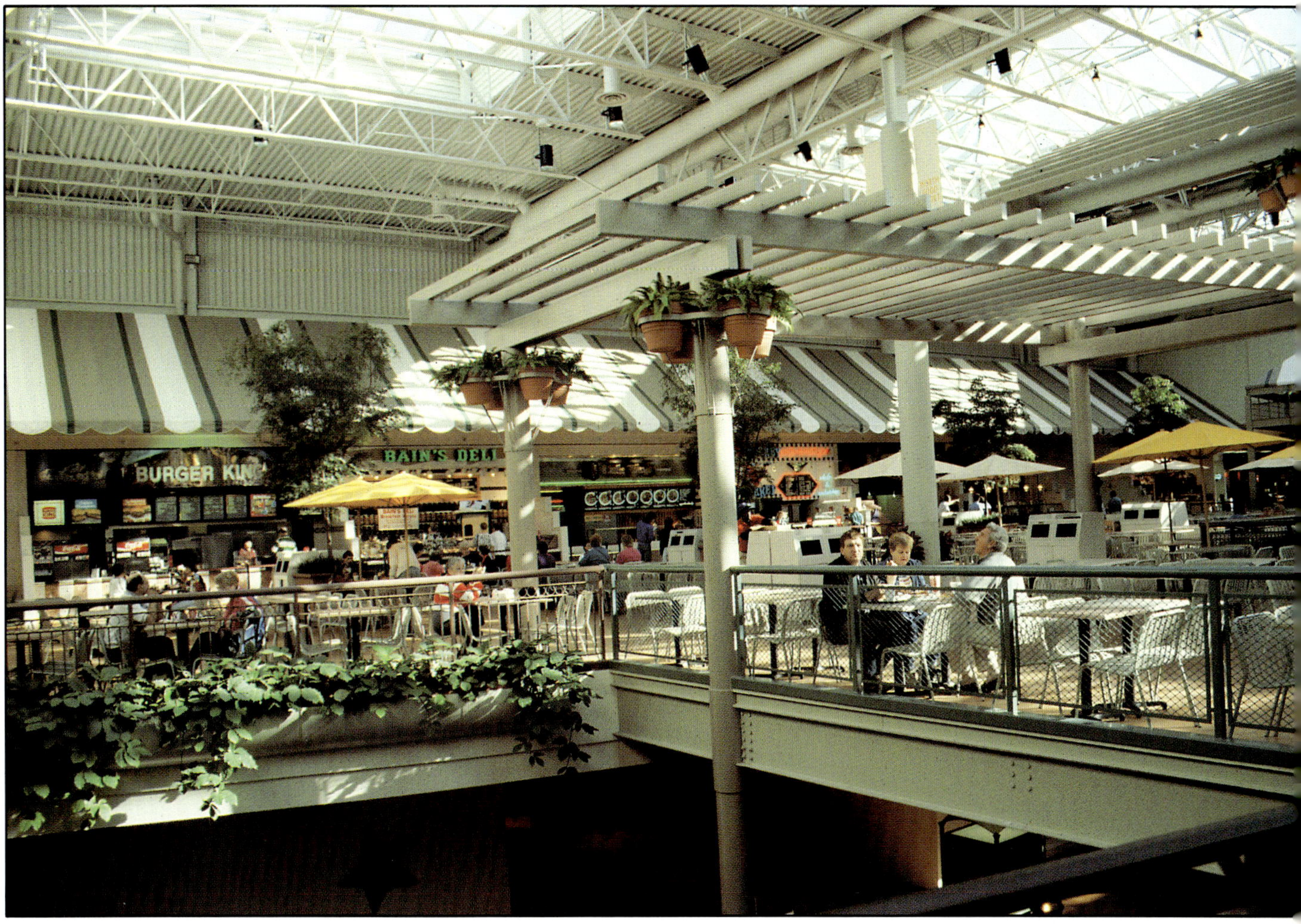
BURGER KING
BAIN'S DELI

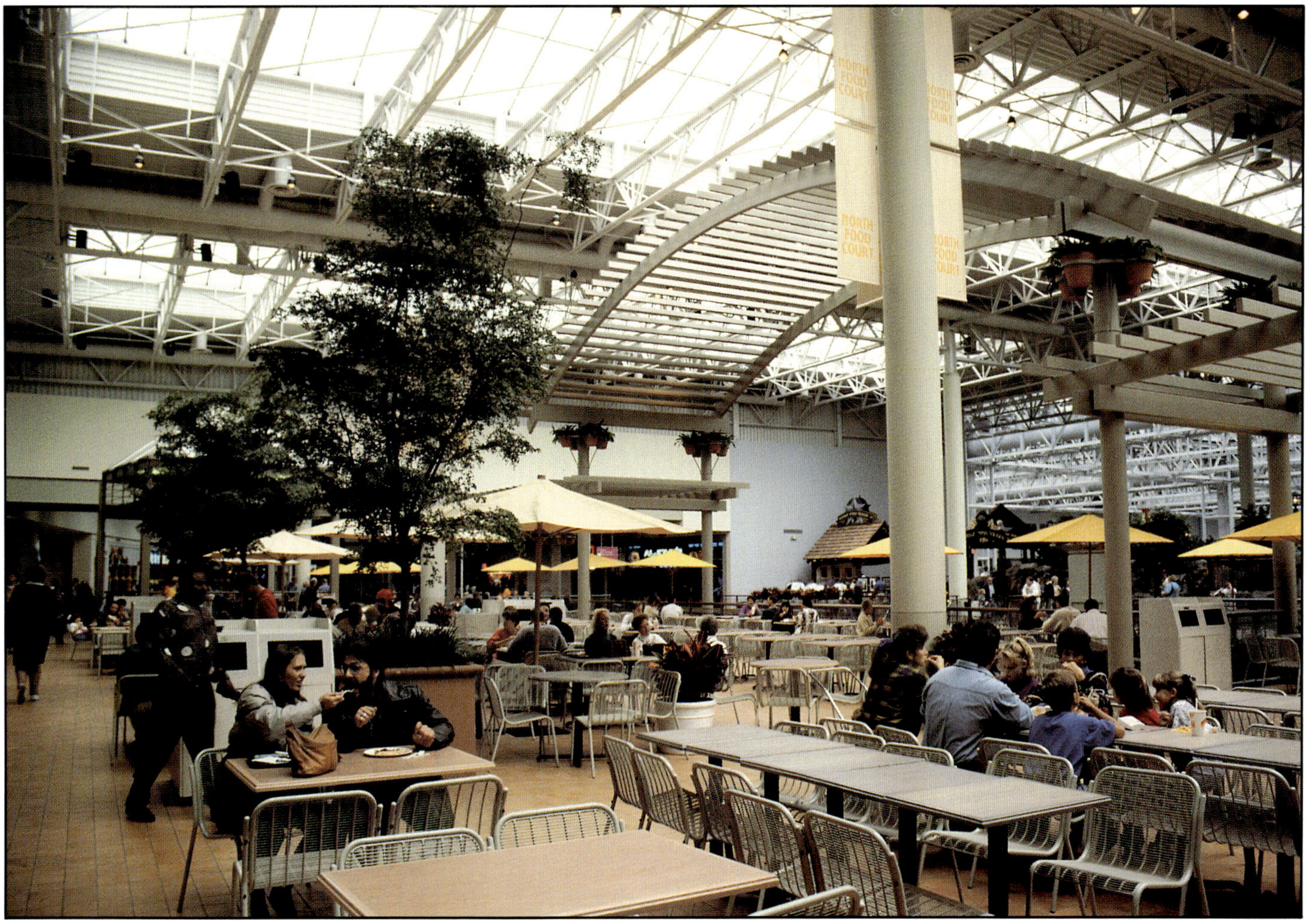
NORTH FOOD COURT

Mall of America

Bloomington, MN

Illustrated here are some of the many fast food concessions that service the diners in the food courts located on the upper levels of South Ave. and North Garden.

Along with the familiar All-American foods such as Great Steak & Fry, Just Turkey (shown later in this chapter), Great American Cookie, Freshems Yogurt, and 1 Potato 2, one of the space's most exciting tenants is Johnny Rockets (below) in the South Ave. F/C. Here, a resemblance to the diners of the '50s is recreated with all the pizzazz and glitter of the original Johnny Rockets Hamburger place on Melrose Ave. in Los Angeles.

Typically local "fare" is served at Minnesota Picnic which in a fun and theatrical manner suggests the Minnesota northlands. Flat cut-out tree silhouettes support a leafy valance over the service counter. The rear wall of the open kitchen is boldly patterned with a checkerboard tile design — like a rustic cotton napkin or tablecloth. The brightly illuminated stand says — "Let's have a picnic" — and Minnesota Picnic has all the fixin's for a great one.

The bottom picture on the opposite page shows a run of food concessions in the North Garden F/C all under a happy colored, flapping yellow awning that unifies them all into one grand smorgasbord.

Photographer: MMP/RVC

Eaton Centre Food Court

Burnaby, Vancouver, BC Canada

The Eaton Centre in Burnaby — just outside of Vancouver — was joined by a second office tower and suddenly the original food court was no longer able to handle the lunch time crowds when office workers and shoppers fought for space — and time. The mall's original food court was expanded 22,000 sq. ft. to include seating for an additional 500 patrons and 12 more food vendors. Currently, the court covers 40,000 sq. ft., seats 1000, and is served by 21 food concessions.

The only available site for the expansion was an area behind the original food court that extends far back from the main pedestrian corridor. The site's awkwardness was compounded by the court's location on the second level of a three-level mall, and there was no opportunity of getting in some natural light.

To attract shoppers and make the food court "a bright, light, and inviting environment for eating and relaxing," a video wall was located near the rear of the new addition — to entice the shoppers and make them come in. Also, there are neon tracings suspended from the ceiling and the neon starts at a sign announcing the food court's presence in the mall's central escalator wall. It then extends through the concourse and all the way back to the new extension. The balance of the lighting is indirect "providing the necessary brightness in a controlled manner which does not lessen the impact of either the video wall or the neon tracings" on the ceiling.

The contemporary design has a high-tech look which complements the existing food court and the design of the mall. It is mainly black and white with bright color accents added to animate the space. The ceiling features large white bulkheads against a black grid pattern, these bulkheads not only break up the expanse of the ceiling, they are also strategically placed above the main aisles to show patrons where to find more seating.

Design: Space Design International, Cincinnati, OH

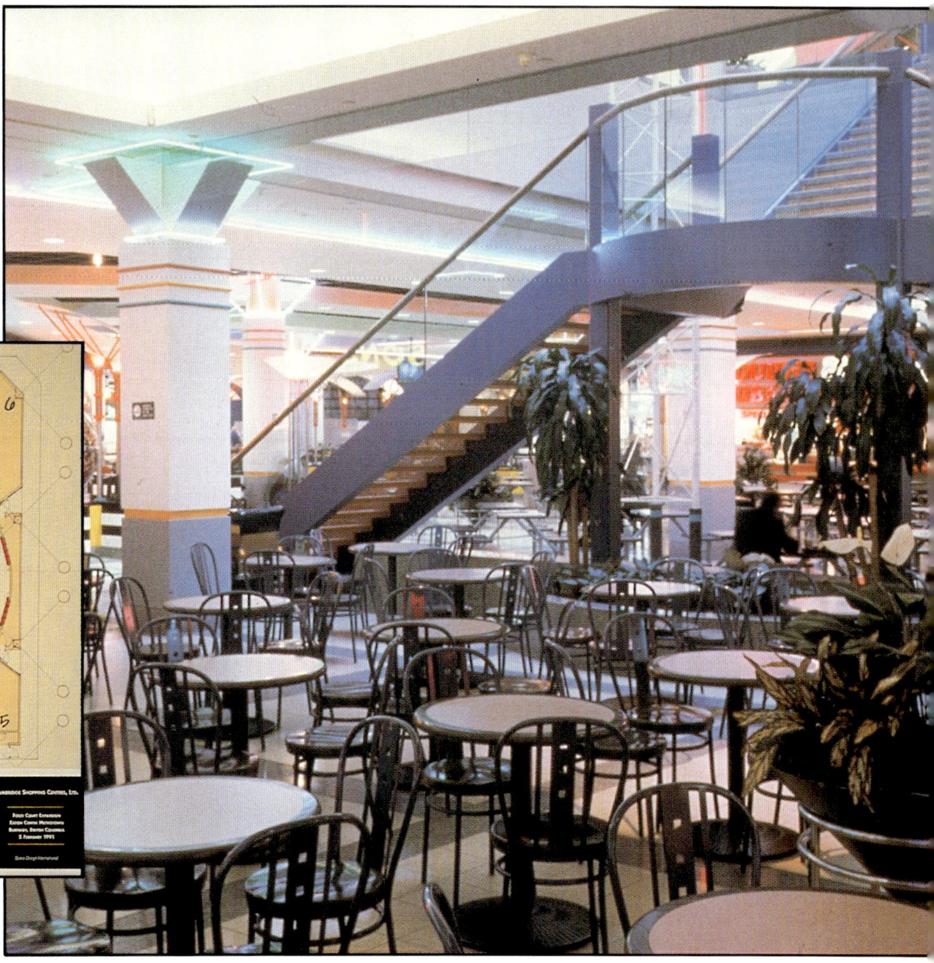

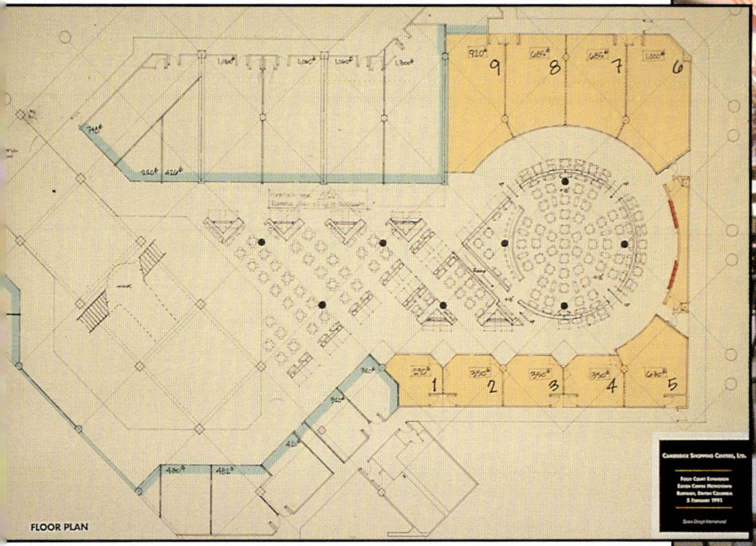
Cambridge Shopping Centres, Ltd.
Food Court Expansion
Eaton Centre Metrotown
Burnaby, British Columbia
5 February 1991
Space Design International

FLOOR PLAN

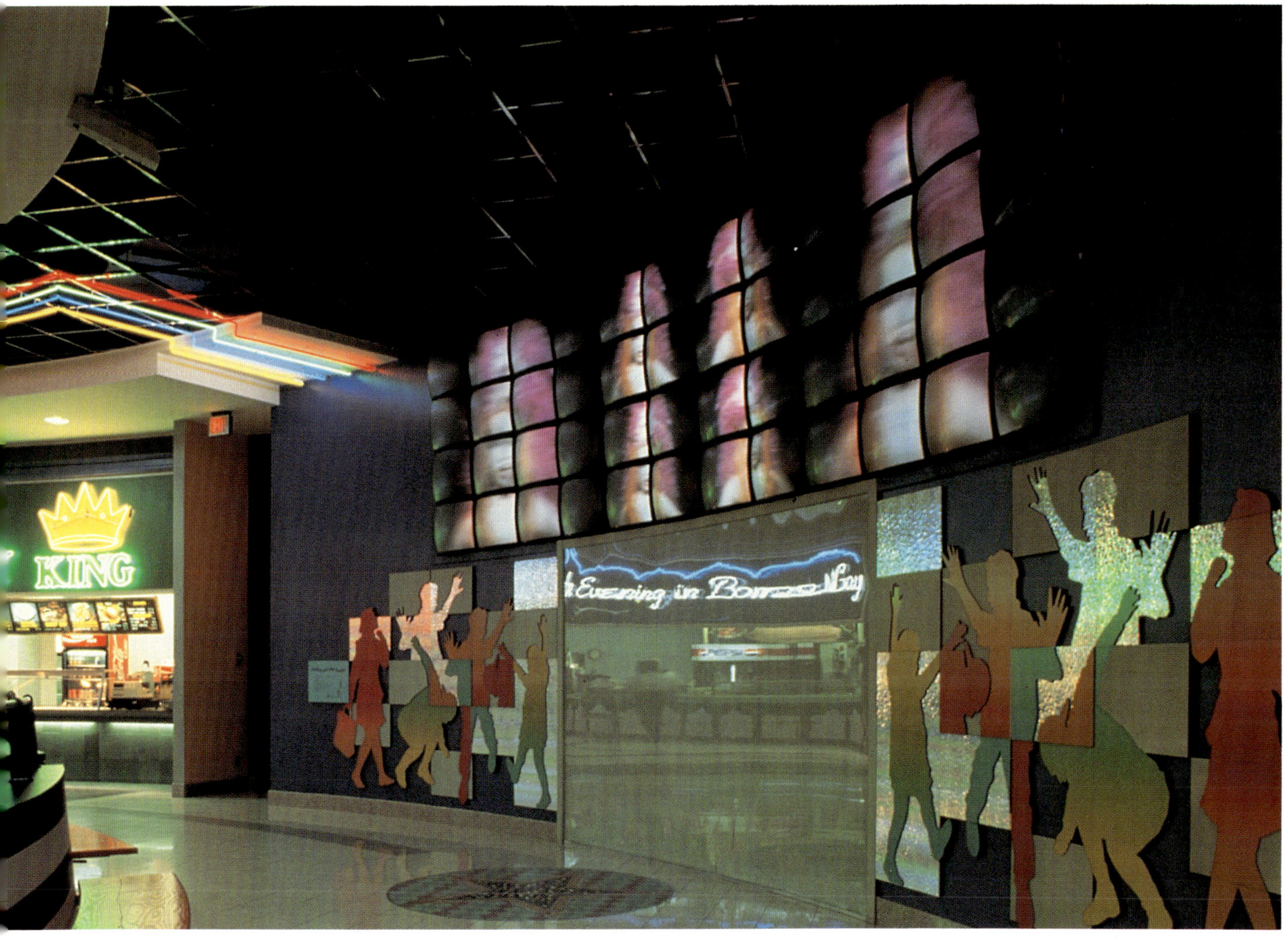
KING
Evening in Bonza Bay

Lakeside Food Court

Thurrock, United Kingdom

Lakeside is a new, large regional shopping centre outside of London. The center is anchored by five large department stores and over 300 other retailers. The 9000 free car parking spaces make this a welcome place to visit since it is so convenient to highway and rail traffic. Once inside — "a highly sophisticated, air-conditioning and computer controlled lighting system maintain a constant, comfortable climate whatever the weather outside."

Palm trees, scenic elevators and escalators and numerous water features also contribute to Lakeside's calm and relaxed atmosphere and the food court is one of the most delightfully relaxing spots in the Centre. The half-round wheel motif with spokes and gilded star logo design announces the location of the food court and the signage is easily located throughout to direct the shoppers up to the upper level where diners can enjoy a variety of international foods in the 600-seat food court. The view of the central atrium, from this vantage point, is worth the trip.

Each concession has its own special look whether it is the red/white/green design on the Pasta & Pizza stand or the Salads & Sandwich concession brimming over with sunshine graphics. Here, freshly-baked breads are combined, to order, with fillings from all over the world. In addition there are Mexican, Chinese, Japanese, Italian, and Nordic specialties available as well as the pub fare — from sizzling breakfasts to roast beef dinners — at English Fayre. For the more youth-oriented crowd, there are Burger King and McDonalds — and much, much more.

A Capital & Countries' Flagship Centre
Photographer: MMP/RVC

Harlequin Shopping Centre
Watford, United Kingdom

Harlequin Shopping Center is located in Central Watford which is not too many miles outside of London. There is a total of 707,000 sq. ft. devoted to retail space and the John Lewis Partnership's Trewin Store takes up another 200,000 sq. ft. of space. The design of this large center has been integrated with some stores who were already there but have expanded their operations in the mall: Marks & Spencers, Littlewoods, and a British Home Store.

Of the 145 smaller retail tenants, the average mall space runs from 500 sq. ft. to 15,000 sq. ft.. The mall was designed to accommodate about 5000 cars in two parking areas; one atop the centre and another adjacent to it. With the mall's location and its access to the M25 and M1 — via the town's ring road — they do draw shoppers from the environs and from London. There is also a British Rail Station nearby.

The mall consists of two trading levels and a basement for the servicing of the mall. It was designed with high, peaked glazed roofs so that daylight can flood the interior spaces. Though the ground level is recessed beneath the second level, there are enough openings in the design where the lower level can also benefit from the daylight. In addition, the mall is "environmentally controlled." and "finished to a very high standard."

Situated on the ground floor is the Food Court. There are seven individually-operated, independent caterers who provide a wide and diverse selection of snacks and meals. The seating can accommodate about 380 persons out in the large open atrium — under the skylight roof and landscaped with plants and trees.

In addition — in the way of amenities — there is a playground located near the Centre manager's office which is fully equipped and monitored, where 3-5 year olds can be left while their parents are off shopping. There is also a Mother's Room where parents can change and feed the infants.

Harlequin Shopping Centre was developed by Capitol Counties plc and Sun Alliance Properties (the property arm of the Sun Alliance Insurance Group) in partnership with the Watford Borough Council.

Architect: Chapman, Taylor Partners
Photographer: MMP/RVC

219

Coronado Cafe

Coronado Center, Albuquerque, NM

The new 20,000 sq. ft. food center was added to the Coronado Center in Albuquerque to help it maintain its position as a premier shopping center and to satisfy its customers' desire for multiple eating options. With a relatively low ceiling (14 ft. at the highest) and no natural light in its lower level location, the space had to be transformed into an attractive, bright and airy environment where up to 325 shoppers could eat, drink, and unwind.

Design: Space Design International, Cincinnati, OH

One of the major design innovations introduced by Space Design International was the creation of ceiling coves with a dramatic, neon-lit, geometric pattern resembling a large starburst. "The highly theatrical ceiling treatment combines architecture and environmental graphics in a 'symbolic' skylight which makes the space appear to be larger and higher than it is." The designers continue the colors of the walls up onto the ceiling so that the two planes seem to merge into one another — visually raising the ceiling. Coves with concealed neon light were also installed around the perimeter walls — to further the feeling of light and spaciousness.

The food court's design also blends a variety of regional styles into a fresh new look that up-dates traditional Southwest themes.

Based on references found in an old Albuquerque theater, the column capitols are fashioned into three dimensional representations of lizards, eagles and snakes. Native American influences can also be seen in the elaborate decorative work that border and trim the flooring, walls, and columns. The intricate tile patterns on the floor and walls and the elaborate ceiling shapes are all influenced by the little known "Pueblo Deco" movement. Also reflecting the local landscape is the color palette of bright sunset colors and the subdued desert tones.

Photographer: MMP/RVC

THE TERRACE
Cortana Mall, Baton Rouge, LA

The new food court in the regional mall on the outer fringe of Baton Rouge seems to have been inspired by the riverboats that used to proudly tour the Mississippi. The half-round, paddle wheel motif is repeated over and over again down the long aisles of the retail area filling in the pronounced half-round arch openings that sectionalize the main aisle.

The food court, the Terrace, is like an outdoor garden with light pouring in from the skylights above the seating area and the dropped pseudo "skylights" that illuminate the seating recessed under the lower ceilings around the "courtyard" which is raised up several steps and is landscaped like a patio. Soaring over this central location are glass and metal barrel vaults that repeat the half round motif again.

The color scheme is mainly composed of a warm rosy peach and a gentle seafoam green accented with a rich, deep green. The floor tiles vary from white accented with the soft Southwest colors to a neutral taupe tile in some of the main walk areas. Plants in the dividing partitions and trees in giant planters landscape the area. The assorted food concessions are lined up along one wall under a striped canvas awning that serves as a bold fascia and destination marker for the hungry shopper.

NORTH SHORE MALL FOOD COURT

Peabody, MA

Design: Arrowsmith Architects, Cambridge, MA
Photographer: Robert E. Micrut Photography

Originally built in 1957 and enclosed in 1976, the North Shore Mall in Peabody, MA has just undergone a major renovation which included the addition of the food court and more leasable square footage.

The formerly drab corridors are now "intimate streets" lined with high fashion shops. The white tiled walkways are patterned with gray and black and accented with garnet colored granite. The bright new arcade alternates between an interior garden with skylights, and planters and a formal hallway of coffered ceilings etched with neon.

The Food Court is less formal than the arcade with festive columns topped by kite-like capitols outlined in neon. Brass, glass, and teal-colored railings rim the outer areas that look down to the new basement level. Custom designed lamps and banners in teal, pink and purple hang from structures of metal and natural wood that are built around some of the columns. "Transformed by the reflective materials on columns and ceilings, these soft colors appear more subtle and fanciful in their myriad variations." Live greenery and trees add a sparkling accent to the skylighted and colorfull Food Court.

Design: *John Herbert Partnership, London, United Kingdom*

Heathrow Food Court

Heathrow Airport, Outside of London, United Kingdom

Food Courts are becoming the popular solution to how to provide multi-food options in public spaces. We are almost shocked when we don't find one in a mall! As we showed in our chapter on Cafeterias, it is not unusual for colleges to provide food courts, of sorts, for the student body. By mixing established fast food operations with specialty food set-ups, Marriott Management Services has successfully solved the problem in colleges and universities.

Heathrow is a giant airport complex that serves London — and is an exit from Europe to the U.S. John Herbert Partnership of London was commissioned to re-design the fast foods and duty free areas in that busy and sprawling airport. In the view shown here, one can see the "mall-like" ambience created with the McDonalds concession lined up and exposed to the heavy traffic aisle. Seating is provided both adjacent and sort of part of McDonalds — on the white tiled floor accented with black squares — and other tables are available further back under the lowered ceiling which is filled with recessed incandescents. Interspersed between the food operations are mini-shops — branches of some of the London shops that the traveler may have missed on the visit to London. They provide something to do besides eating while waiting — and they further enhance the "food court" ambience.

Westminister Mall Food Court

Westminister, CA

The project for the design firm of Corbin/Yamafuji & Partners of Irvine, CA was to revitalize the design of the mid-'70s mall and create a central location for the 20,000 sq. ft. food court.

Design: Corbin/Yamafuji and Partners, Irvine, CA

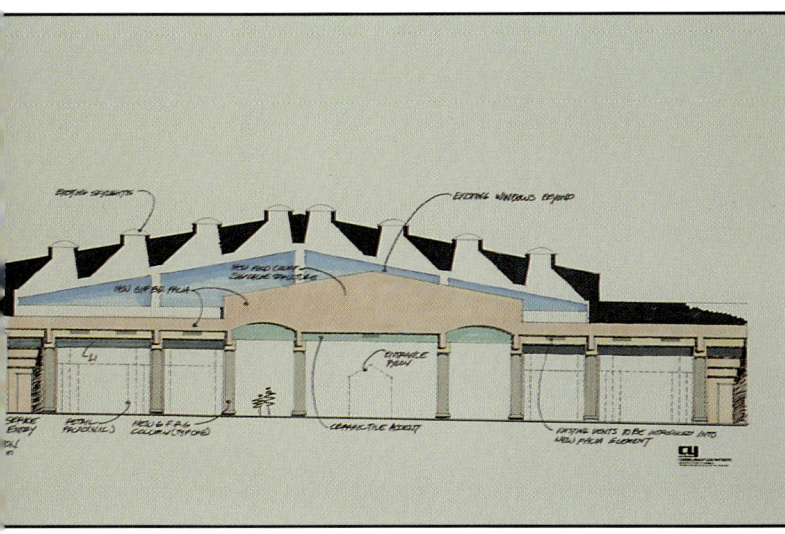

A series of columns are used to identify and illuminate the circular dining area which is located beneath a crown-like sky-lit rotunda. It was designed to be an inviting retreat from the main promenade. Radiating out from the rotunda and under the lower ceiling surrounding the open seating area are the assorted food services which offer snacks and light food options. Though most of the diners prefer the light, airy and spacious central seating area with its generous landscaping, there are additional tables provided in uniquely designed niches adjacent to the food service areas.

"The design creates an animated environment throughout these spaces enhanced by the consistent signage and contemporary colors."

Design: The Company

AUNTIE ANNE'S
Exton Square Mall, Exton, PA

This relatively new fast food operation out of Pennsylvania is staking out its position in food courts in Pennsylvania and Delaware and it is sure to become a favorite with pretzel lovers everywhere.

The big attraction is watching the young people in their blue and white checkerboard bordered aprons and hats rolling, cutting, and twisting the individual soft pretzels which can be baked to order; with or without salt; with or without butter; sweet or regular. In addition to the pretzel logo and the Auntie Anne's sign in light blue neon on the white fascia overhead, the blue and white checkerboard motif appears on all the paper goods, napkins and packaging — and makes its biggest impact as the decorative border across the white tiled front of the concession. The same warm blue is used as an accent amidst all the white in the open, functional bakery/prep area beyond. The pretzels are baked in the stainless steel ovens while a white marble surface — up front, behind glass, serves as the "theater" where the pretzel makers do their twists and turns.

KITCHENS OF BAY STATE

Prudential Center, Boston, MA

The upper part of this fast food service operation's facade recalls the waves that are associated with bays. Undulating forms of assorted blue and blue/green corrugated metal sweep around over the blue and white checkerboard valance of the shop. "Kitchens of the" is in gold applied letters over one of the waves while "Bay State" is in white and contained in a blue oval outlined in white.

The shop itself is basically orange and blue plus aqua and white, and accents of light natural wood for trim. The lower part of the glazed facade are blocked off with large orange squares while the soffit over the blue backed prep area repeats the orange and white checkerboard pattern. The long service counter that angles its way through the space is faced with a white striated laminate and framed and topped with the reddish brown wood. Aqua and blue corrugated panels — like those used on the exterior — appear over the orange/white pattern to continue the watery motif. Dimensional gold letters and stars — like those that provide the signage on the facade — are used on a blue fascia to indicate the menu selections.

The floor is laid with tiles of aqua, blue, pink, and white in a non-directional, random design — on an angle across the space. In addition to the large, white dome-shaped pendant lamps over the counter, white spot holders follow the perimeter walls and light up the menu boards and the chalk board specials.

Design: Judd Brown Designs, Warwick, RI
Graphics: Hunter Signs

KFC

Eaton Center, Toronto, Ontario, Canada

The red diagonal stripes that are part of the KFC logo on the very recognizable buckets of Kentucky Fried Chicken also appear prominently in this new KFC store in the Eaton Centre in Toronto. The motif appears on the facade where the stripes start as fins — at grade level — and subsequently they rise through the exterior of the ground floor, the interior of the second floor, and outside again where they pierce through the roof.

The designers, Nowski Partners Architects, also use the take-out bucket's shape as a source of inspiration. They carved the facade inwards from the street. This meant a renovation of an existing building and therefore, only the ground floor could curve inwards for structural reasons. This helped to also increase the number of window seats available so that more patrons could watch the aisle traffic outside and it also created "a lobster-trip like entrance. By the time you reach the entry doors you have already been pulled one third of the distance to the rear order counter and kitchen — 80 ft. from the street."

The color and materials palette — like the logo — emphasizes the shade of red in a white, gray, and black interior.

Design: Nowski Partners, Architects, Willowdale, Ontario, Canada
Partner in Charge: Jim Nowski
Project Architect: John Moses
Designer in Charge: Colin Kingsland
Designer: Wiszula Tokarska
Photographer: Tony Whibley, UFX Projections, Inc.

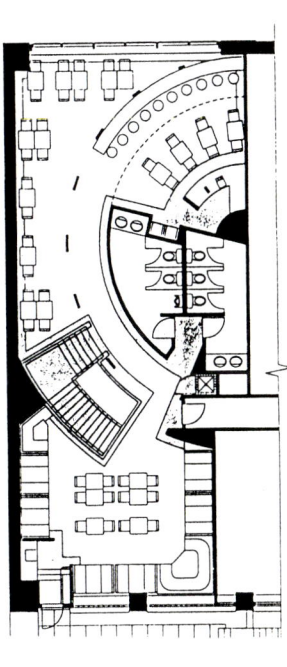

JUST TURKEY
Mall of America, Bloomington, MN

One of the food attractions in the garden-like setting of the North Garden Food Court is Just Turkey. The white tiled counter and back wall are set off with red, yellow, blue, and black tiles and also lines of sizzling neon. The sliced meats and prepared salads are displayed in glass fronted cases to either side of the service counter area which is glistening white like the tiles all around it. Directly over the stainless rotisserie on the rear, exposed wall is the shop's logo; a red heart shaped turkey surrounded by "Just Turkey" in a sharp, cool blue color.

The black menu boards on the white tiled walls are outlined with red neon and up above — red neon also describes the stands specialties. Red and blue neon "feathers" also highlight the good-for-your-heart turkey motif. The space and the menu boards are brilliantly illuminated by spot lights that extend out from off the rear wall of the stand. Like the concessions that neighbor Just Turkey, a yellow canvas awning runs the length of the stands unifying them into a single entity.

Photographer: MMP/RVC

Design: Vinick Associates, Hartford, CT
Photographer: Warren Jagger

BOSTON CHICKEN
Cromwell, CT

The problem facing Vinick Associates, the designers, was how to transform a typical strip center location into "a functional and cozy retail store with dining space."

Millwork was added to the store front to create a more homey or residential look with multi-paned windows. Inside the natural maple millwork and shelves help to break up the back counter area into "smaller visual elements. This helps reduce the space to a human and 'residential' scale." Elements like the decorative maple shelving, the coat rack and display armoire (which houses the refuse and the recyclable containers) add to the warm ambience. Copper panels camouflage the exhaust hoods and the menu boards on the teal fascia are also framed in the light, natural maple.

In the dining area, a gray/green wall covering patterned in white is applied over the maple chair rail, and a paler green material is used as a frieze under the ceiling line. Gray/green accents are found along the front line, as accent tiles, and on the hanging light fixtures. Peach and beige flashed and textured ceramic tiles are laid on the floor.

"The overall goal of creating a homey — 'come to my kitchen' atmosphere is achieved through the use of durable finishes that still have a 'residential' feel."

Pizza Pizzaz

Harlem Irving Pl., Norridge, IL

This 1200 sq. ft. prototype was designed to create "an image of quality" — focusing on freshly prepared food in a fast food restaurant of small size, without seating, in a mall environment.

The designer, Phillip M. LeBoy, used color and brightness — highlighted with accent illumination to intensify the overall image and product presentation, and also to help this concession space stand out in a realm where color and brightness are the norm. Super graphics were also developed to visually present the food while also attracting the customer. The graphics and signage was well designed as the menu boards are all very readable and color coordinated with the overall decorating scheme. "They have been created as part of the design — not as an attachment."

Working with quality materials like brass and marble, the designer in close coordination with the owner, developed a front line counter display which includes displays of fresh ingredients laid upon beds of lettuce around the trays of food for serving. "Food retailing has, to a great extent, become one of demonstration and pizzaz." Showing the customer the use of the fresh ingredients and preparation, with the display of the final product done in the highest quality of sensory presentation makes for a successful restaurant," says Phillip LeBoy.

Design: Phillip M. LeBoy Architects, AIA, P.C., Skokie, IL

Design: *Phillip M. LeBoy Architects, Skokie, IL*

SUBS 'N' SALADS

Orland Square, Orland Park, IL

Squeezed in between other food services in the Orland Square Food Court is Subs 'n' Salads. The designer, Phillip M. LeBoy, designed this stand with bright colors used in a "straightforward manner."

Blue and yellow ceramic tiles are checkerboarded across the service counter and the front has an under-lighted counter edge as well as an under-lighted toe space so that it seems to "float" off the brown tiled floor of the food court. The same primary colored tiles create a decorative band across the white tiled wall of the prep/kitchen area. The counter top is "lettuce green" and translucent glass blocks are used on a portion of the counter to shield the work surface. Stainless steel is used as a background and hood over the grill and cooking area.

The right hand side of the counter is the "salad" section and the neon sign on the stainless hood brings the customer to the display of fresh ingredient bins which are under glass.

A white canvas awning projects forward towards the mall and it is brightly illuminated from within so that the all-important name and colorful graphics literally glow in the darkness over the stand.

PECOS BILL'S
Tucson Mall Food Court, Tucson, AZ

This fast food concession in the Tucson Mall features Texas-style barbecue. To identify the stand and the type of food, the designer, Rafique Islam of Sixty First Pl. Architects decided on a totally Texan motif which starts with the colors and design of the Lone Star state flag which wraps across the serving counter in red, white, and blue. The rear wall of the preparation area is covered with a quilted pattern of stainless steel while a sweeping fascia on top carries a series of TV monitors playing country and western music videos and a back-lighted menu board.

In keeping with the Texan menu, sheriff's badges are embedded into the serving counter and longhorns are attached to the poles that support the sneeze guard. Pecos Bill — riding a tornado — sits in a white plate set against a provincial, country-style red and white checkered tablecloth. Behind the name is a map of Texas.

This striking and illuminated graphic/logo is located on the cashier's wall — just above eye level, and a fitting exclamation point to the music videos/signboard fascia that caps the space.

Design: Sixty First Pl. Architects, Scottsdale, AZ
Photographer: Rafique Islam

Taquito's

Los Arcos Mall, Scottsdale, AZ

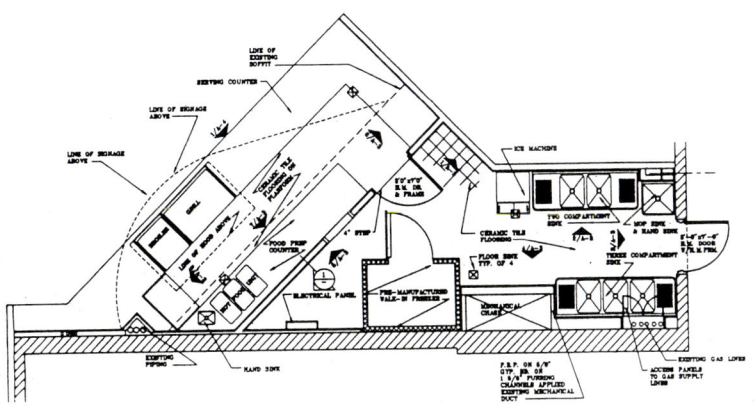

Taquito's is a Mexican fast food stand located in the Los Arcos food court and there are several more Taquito's located in the Southwest area. The preparation of the familiar and spicy foods are presented up front above the Mexican tiles that are used to face the counter with the zig zag motif. The red, white, and green tiles are the colors that appear in the Mexican flag and the stepped motif suggests Aztec temple structures or zuggurats. The same three colors are used to stripe the rear wall of the stand which is faced with white tiles. The grill occupies a major portion of the front counter and it becomes an important part of the design of the space. The hood above is covered with plaster in the form of a giant taco shell.

The soffit is treated with "Southwest" colors and bright pink, yellow, and blue neon are used for the signs and the logo that distinguishes Taquito's.

Design: Sixty First Pl. Architects, Scottsdale, AZ
Photographer: Rafique Islam

ABOUT THE EDITOR

Martin M. Pegler has long been considered a leading authority on store design and visual merchandising. He has been involved in the field for almost forty years and has worked in all phases of merchandise presentation: designer, manufacturer, display person, store planner and consultant. Witty, urbane, erudite and most persuasive, he has long been a vocal champion of store design and visual presentation as a necessary and respected part of retailing. This has made him a popular speaker across the country and for two tours of the British Isles, Mexico and Japan. He is in demand as a lecturer for industry, small business groups as well as, nation-wide chains and shopping centers.

Mr. Pegler is author of *Successful Food Merchandising & Display, Stores of the Year, Store Windows That Sell, Food Presentation & Display, Home Furnishings Merchandising & Store Design,* and *Market Supermarket & Hypermarket Design.*

He is currently a professor of Store Planning and Visual Merchandising at the Fashion Institute of Technology in New York and travels extensively, — always searching the field for new and fresh approaches, ideas and techniques to share.

A
Abda Market, 16
Agatha & Valentina, 20
Airstreams Roadside Diner, 120
American University Food Court, 113
Anthropologie, 78
Aromaz Coffee and PastryBar, 58
Auntie Anne's, 228
Azzuro, 170

B
Barnie's, 60
Barnie's Kiosks & Carts, 62
Ben's Deli, 12
Bistro 89, 144
Bistro 110, 157
Blue Note Bar, 80
Boston Chicken, 233
Boulder's Bakery/Cafe, 45
Busketti Boy, 178

C
Cafe Briacco, 94
Cafe Med at Cocowalk, 126
Cafe Nina, 83
Cafe Pacifica, 200
Cafe Tazza, 84
Cafe Un Deux Trois, 156
California State University Cafeteria, 112
Carmine's, 166
Champion Brew Pub, 158
Charcuterie Traiteur, 34
Checkers, 139
Chex Gerard, 146
Children's Way Cafeteria, 117
Chocolate Chariot, 46
Ciao Baby Cucina, 162
Clay Pit, 192
Confetti Chocolat, 47
Coronado Cafe, 220

D
Denver Salad Bar, 98
Deutsches Museum Cafe, 74
Deutsches Museum Cafeteria, 90
Dolce & Freddo, 115
Dos Hermanos, 180

E
Eaton Centre Food Court, 214
Eccola, 172
Eurasia, 199

F
Felissimo Tea Room, 81
Flo Prestige, 35
Food Garden Cafe, 102

G
General Accident Insurance Co. Cafeteria, 116

H
Harlequin Shopping Centre, 218
Harvey Nichols-Fifth Floor, 72
Harvey Nichols Market, 30
Heartwise Express, 130
Heathrow Food Court, 225
Heissenberger Tea & Coffee, 64
Herald Cafe, 109
Honrura-An, 202
Hundertwasser Museum Cafe, 76

I
Il Fornaio Cucina Expressa, 92
Indiana State University Food Court, 110
Island Market, 22

J
Java Express, 63
J.F.F. Kettunen, 155
Joe Rockheads, 134
Jonathan Morr Espresso Bar, 86
Just Turkey, 232

K
Ka De We Cafes, 70
Käfer, 27
Kappeli, 82
Kelley & Ping, 38
KFC, 231
Kin Khao, 194
Kinetsu Bistro/Cafe, 79
Kintetsu Market, 28
Kitchens of Bay State, 229
Knott's Berry Farm Market, 40

L
La Parrilla Suiza, 179
Lakeside Food Court, 216
L'Epicure, 66
Local-No Chol, 132
Loeb's Bakery, 42

M
Maison du Fromage, 37
Mall of America, 212
Mall of America Food Courts, 210
Mi Piace, 152
Mia Torre, 168
Morton's of Chicago, 149

N
Nasch Markt, 18
Neuman & Bogdonoff, 24
New World Coffee, 56
Newsbar, 68
North Shore Mall Food Court, 224

O
Ollie's, 188

P
Panorama, 190
Papa Razzi, 174
Papi Luis Cafe, 87
Pasadena Baking Co., 44
Pasqua Coffee Bars, 52
Patio Coffee Shop, 151
Pecos Bill's, 236
P.F. Chang's, 185
Pizza Pizzaz, 234

R
Rumpel Markt, 32

S
Salad Bowl, 96
Sandwich Box, 106
Seattle Coffee Roasters, 54
Soho Soho, 140
Sony Music Center Cafeteria, 114
Sony Sushi Club, 204
Souper Salads, 100
Spinnakers, 136
State Fare Food Court, 208
Subs 'n' Salads, 235

T
Tang's Ginger Cafe, 186
Taquito's, 237
Tessi, 36
The Earth, 124
The Good Diner, 128
The Good Earth, 108
The Terrace, 223
Tres Lobos, 182
Tosca, 164

V
Vivo, 176
Vong, 196

W
Westminister Mall Food Court, 226
Winter Garten, 104

Y
Yellow Rose Cafe, 122

Z
Zoë, 142